Student Handbook to Sociology

Research Methods

Volume II

Student Handbook to Sociology

Research Methods

Volume II

AMY DONLEY

Liz Grauerholz
General Editor

Facts On File

An Infobase Learning Company

Student Handbook to Sociology: Research Methods
Copyright © 2012 Amy Donley

Facts On File, Inc.
An Imprint of Infobase Learning
132 West 31st Street
New York NY 10001

Library of Congress Cataloging-in-Publication Data

Student handbook to sociology / Liz Grauerholz, general editor.
  v. cm.
  Includes bibliographical references and index.
  Contents: v. 1. History and theory—v. 2. Research methods—v. 3. Social structure—v. 4. Socialization—v. 5. Stratification and inequality—v. 6. Deviance and crime—v. 7. Social change.
  ISBN 978-0-8160-8314-5 (alk. paper)—ISBN 978-0-8160-8315-2 (v. 1 : alk. paper)—ISBN 978-0-8160-8316-9 (v. 2 : alk. paper)—ISBN 978-0-8160-8317-6 (v. 3 : alk. paper)—ISBN 978-0-8160-8319-0 (v. 4 : alk. paper)—ISBN 978-0-8160-8320-6 (v. 5 : alk. paper)—ISBN 978-0-8160-8321-3 (v. 6 : alk. paper)—ISBN 978-0-8160-8322-0 (v. 7 : alk. paper)
  1. Sociology. I. Grauerholz, Elizabeth, 1958–
  HM585.S796 2012
  301—dc23   2011025983

Facts On File books are available at special discounts when purchased in bulk quantities for businesses, associations, institutions, or sales promotions. Please call our Special Sales Department at (212) 967-8800 or (800) 322-8755.

You can find Facts On File on the World Wide Web at
http://www.infobaselearning.com

Text design by Erika K. Arroyo
Composition by Kerry Casey
Cover printed by Yurchak Printing, Landisville, Pa.
Book printed and bound by Yurchak Printing, Landisville, Pa.
Date Printed: April 2012
Printed in the United States of America

10 9 8 7 6 5 4 3 2 1

This book is printed on acid-free paper.

CONTENTS

FOREWORD

Every time you log onto the Internet, watch television, or open a magazine, you are bombarded with social "facts" and claims: "One in two marriages ends in divorce!" "Alabama changed the value of pi to 3 to be consistent with biblical teachings!" "Halloween candy poses serious risks to children!" "Underwire bras cause breast cancer!" "Illegal immigrants are putting undue pressure on our health care and educational systems!" "Humans use only 10 percent of their brain!" "Domestic oil drilling will solve our energy crisis!"

Near constant access to facts and data that are available 24/7 has resulted in information overload. If you Google the word "cancer" you get over 81 million hits. How can you possibly know which ones are legitimate and which ones are not? How do you know if the data reported in the story you read are fabricated or derived from systematic research? Is this just someone's opinion or is there something to back it up? It doesn't help that it has become increasingly more difficult to distinguish between legitimate news sources and those whose jobs are to entertain or sell, or are clearly biased.

With so much information, including harmful and often false claims about people and groups, it has become imperative that we understand how to sort fact from fiction. It is not too far-fetched to state that the health of our country as a democracy depends upon our ability to do so. Indeed, a poorly informed or misinformed public is likely to be easily swayed by those who sound convincing. Those who believe that nearly all claims are equally valid will feel overwhelmed; those who think that you can't believe anything you hear or read may avoid participating in the democratic process and abandon social causes, even those injustices about which they feel most strongly. Without the tools to make sense of all the facts and information you are exposed to daily, it is hard to muster up the concern or energy to exercise your democratic responsibilities.

One of the main reasons for acquiring a solid understanding of social methodology is that it helps you learn to question what you hear, read, or even see. Research skills and knowledge, coupled with a sociological perspective, provide the tools for evaluating information for its veracity. Rather than accept all claims as true or reject all claims as outright lies or attempts at manipulation, you learn to ask questions that allow you to make informed and discerning decisions. A sociological perspective, in short, can help you be a better citizen.

This volume provides you with vital tools that will help you make sense of the social world. You will learn about the many ways sociologists have come to learn about the social world—from observations of people in their natural environment to large-scale surveys of a nation's citizens. You will also learn about the importance of research ethics, information that will teach you how to conduct ethical research, help you distinguish between appropriate and inappropriate methods, and enable you to evaluate risks and benefits associated with the methods you are considering. The information presented here will give you the skills to conduct your own research, which is the next step in thinking like and becoming a sociologist.

—Liz Grauerholz, University of Central Florida

INTRODUCTION

Sociology is concerned with society and the interactions between people. Because sociology is interested in all facets of the social world, potential research topics are seemingly limitless. Sociologists study groups of people, like families and gangs; social problems, like poverty and drug abuse; social inequality, which arises from race, class and gender differences; social institutions, like education and religion; and social movements, such as the Civil Rights movement and the environmental movement. This list is far from exhaustive. Basically if it concerns people and the society in which we live, sociologists are probably studying it!

We often study topics that people may hold strong opinions about. But sociology is not about opinions and does not consist of just looking at the world around us. Sociology is a science. Sociologists strive to be objective when studying social phenomenon, basing their conclusions on research findings. Sociology relies on the same general scientific method used in other areas of science with which you are no doubt familiar. However, because sociology is concerned with the social world, sociologists use a variety of methods specifically tailored to provide a better understanding of the world in which we live and the interactions between and among people. This volume explores many of the different methods that sociologists use to conduct research in the social world.

Research typically follows a basic study path. We formulate questions and develop plans that allow us to answer these questions. We build on the work of others while seeking new ways to explore, examine, and understand social issues. We rely on a variety of research methods to collect data. While there are exceptions and variations to this pattern, it provides a basic roadmap for research.

The many research methods used in sociology fall under two main categories: quantitative and qualitative. Some sociologists conduct research using only quantitative methods while others use only qualitative methods. One approach is not better than the other. They involve different techniques and the result is different types of data. They can also answer different questions. There are benefits and consequences associated with all of the various research methods. The hope is that that you will appreciate both general types of research for how they can illuminate issues in which we are interested.

A core concern in conducting research is doing so in an ethical way. Although sociologists don't conduct medical tests on people, we do often ask people about sensitive topics and this can lead to emotional and psychological distress. We also seek information that could be potentially damaging if it were released publicly. Because of these and other reasons that are discussed in this book, ethics are a core concern for researchers. Several of the most famous examples of unethical behavior in research are described, examples that clearly show that just because something is legal does not necessarily make it ethical and that what is considered "unethical" is often debatable.

Without getting bogged down in what are often complicated statistical models, this volume will explain many of the core concepts used in research and address the question: How do we know what we know? As a society, we are confronted with statistics and claims about social reality all of the time. Sociologists (or students learning to think in a sociological way) ask questions about such claims. When confronted, for example, with a fairly common assertion that half of all marriages end in divorce, a sociologist asks, "How do you know that?" This volume will also explain how sociologists come to the conclusions that they reach and introduce you to methods that will allow you to better question what you hear about our world. Thinking in a sociological way and understanding the research methods and concepts explained in this volume can also make you a more informed and conscientious consumer of information.

Finally, this volume will provide guidelines for conducting your own sociological research study. Although there may be no such thing as a perfect research study, decades of research have taught us a lot about how to conduct good studies. This section of the book will serve as a guide for young researchers eager to conduct their own examinations of the social world.

CHAPTER 1

THE ROLE OF RESEARCH METHODS IN SOCIOLOGY

All members of all societies make observations about their social worlds. You no doubt have done so yourself, on countless occasions. You may have noticed a homeless person sleeping on the street and wondered how that person became homeless. You may have noticed that the majority of the teachers in your elementary school were women and wondered why that is the case. Or you may have heard about a social group or political movement in your community and wondered what motivates people to join.

"Thinking like a sociologist" is not only noticing what is going on around you but also wondering why things are the way they are. A sociologist sees a homeless person and wonders, "How many people are homeless and how do they end up living on the streets?" Another might observe that most elementary school teachers are women and wonder about the social processes that produce gender segregation in the workplace. A third notices people joining social groups and speculates on their reasons for doing so.

HOW SOCIOLOGICAL RESEARCH IS UNIQUE

Sociologist C. Wright Mills coined the term **sociological imagination** to refer to the process of thinking about the connections between the things we have experienced and the larger society in which we live. Sociology, in short, is concerned with the connection between the individual and the larger society. As

Mills observed, "Neither the life of an individual nor the history of a society can be understood without understanding both."

While all people make observations about their social world and speculate on why things are as they are, sociologists try to be systematic in both their observations and in the related speculations. Systematic observation is called **research**; systematic speculation is called **theory**. By "systematic" we mean that the observation and speculation is done methodically, according to a plan. True science, whether social or natural, involves deriving propositions from theory and testing those propositions with research. Through scientific research, we come to theoretical generalizations about how the social world is organized.

Sociologists seek answers to questions about the social world by conducting scientific research. For sociologists, this research does not usually occur in a laboratory but rather in the "real world." Society is a sociologist's laboratory. It is where we conduct studies that connect what individuals experience with the larger society. Most people use their own personal experiences to come to conclusions about what is true in society at large. But personal experience is often extremely atypical and therefore provides a very poor basis for generalization. People may be quick to point to their own experiences as "evidence" that something works or is correct. But anecdotal evidence, while at times interesting and even insightful, is far from systematic. The entire point of social research is to transcend personal experience and base one's generalizations on scientifically valid data. How such data comes to be produced is what this book is about.

This is not to say that personal experience has no place in science. To the contrary, researchers are often drawn to areas of research because of their own experiences. For example, sociologist Dalton Conley has conducted research on race in America—no doubt an interest rooted in Conley's childhood, which involved growing up as a white person in a predominantly black housing project in New York City. Personal experience, however, is not a prerequisite for selecting an area of research. For example, many sociologists who conduct research on domestic violence are not themselves survivors of domestic violence; most researchers who study poverty and homelessness have never been poor or homeless themselves; and many sociologists who study religion are themselves agnostic in their religious beliefs. Sociologists are drawn to certain areas of inquiry for many different reasons and there is no "right" reason to study any particular topic or issue.

Just as there are many aspects of social life, so too are there many areas of specialization within sociology. There are sociologists who study the family, others who focus on poverty and inequality, still others who conduct research on social mobility, and so on. Researchers immerse themselves in a particular topic so they will be aware of what we already know about the topic and

American Sociological Association

The American Sociological Association (ASA), which is the national professional organization for sociologists, currently has 49 sections. Sections are specialization areas with which members can associate. Within each section are other sociologists who specialize in the same area. The current sections in the ASA are listed below.

Aging and the Life Course

Alcohol, Drugs, and Tobacco

Altruism, Morality, and Social Solidarity

Animals and Society

Asia and Asian America

Body and Embodiment

Children and Youth

Collective Behavior & Social Movements

Communication and Information Technologies

Community and Urban Sociology

Comparative and Historical Sociology

Crime, Law, and Deviance

Culture

Disability and Society

Economic Sociology

Education

Emotions

Environment and Technology

Ethnomethodology and Conversation Analysis

Evolution, Biology, and Society

Family

Global and Transnational Sociology

History of Sociology

Human Rights

International Migration

Labor and Labor Movements

Latino/a Sociology

Law

Marxist Sociology

Mathematical Sociology

Medical Sociology

Mental Health

Methodology

Organizations, Occupations, and Work

Peace, War, and Social Conflict

Political Economy of the World System

Political Sociology

Population

Race, Gender, and Class

Racial and Ethnic Minorities

Rationality and Society

Religion

Science, Knowledge, and Technology

Sex and Gender

Sexualities

Social Psychology

Sociological Practice and Public Sociology

Teaching and Learning

Theory

what we do not yet know. The things not yet known in turn become the objects or focus of research. In general, the same concepts, principles, and procedures of research are employed regardless of the subject under investigation. These concepts, principles, and procedures are the "scientific method" as applied to sociological research.

What sets sociological research apart from the casual observations made by lay people is that sociological research is conducted in a systematic and rigorous way. Consider, for example, the way television reporters commonly report on a news story. They will often interview one or two people to get a reaction to some newsworthy event. Suppose a school district is considering changing the time that schools operate. A reporter may interview a parent sitting in the car pick up line waiting for his or her child to get out of school. Quite often, one or two of these interviews is presented as "parents' reaction to the proposed change." Clearly this is not a systematic assessment of how all or even most parents of children enrolled in the district's schools feel about the issue. It is the reaction of two people, at one school, who both pick up their children. Are these two parents indicative of all of the parents whose children attend schools in the district? Their reactions may or may not be the same as the reactions of other parents who pick up their children, parents of children that ride the bus home, or parents whose children stay at the school for after care.

In sociological research the idea is not just to observe a few instances of a phenomenon or ask a couple people their views. Instead, research methods are used to get an accurate picture of what is really going on. This is what sets sociology apart from casual speculation. Conducting research in a systematic way requires a knowledge of research principles. These principles guide the researcher through the process of coming to conclusions about the social world that are not based on anecdote or personal experience but are based on scientific inquiry.

One core concern in conducting systematic research is reducing bias. **Bias** refers to the undue influence of what should be extraneous factors in the research process. Bias can come in many forms and in all stages in the research process: in selecting participants, in data collection, and in the interpretation of results. Bias must be avoided to ensure that findings are an accurate representation of reality. There are many types of bias; several of the more common ones will be discussed in depth in Chapter 7. For now it is sufficient to state that researchers must, if and when possible, prevent bias from influencing their research at all stages.

The 19th century German sociologist Max Weber and many others have advocated for value neutrality in sociology, which means eliminating all personal biases, preconceived notions, ideologies, and prejudices to the greatest extent possible in every aspect of research. Obviously, research will have more credibility if the results are not biased by personal feelings and political motivations. When the National Rifle Association publishes the results of its latest gun control poll, people opposed to the association's position on gun control (and perhaps many others) do not take them seriously; by the same token, one must question the objectivity of poll results produced by groups on the other side of the issue. Still, many have argued that being completely value neutral is impossible and that all research is biased to some degree. Nevertheless, value neutrality remains the goal when conducting research. Most researchers strive to be objective and to acknowledge their own biases just so their results can be properly evaluated. Completely setting aside one's preconceived notions, values, and world outlooks may well be impossible, but the basic argument for value neutrality, advocated by Weber and others, remains valid: Social scientists should not openly advocate for their personal views on matters of social fact and should make every effort not to let their observations and conclusions be influenced by their preconceived ideas. This is a goal pursued by most sociologists, albeit with varying degrees of success.

WHY DO RESEARCH?

Just as there are many areas of sociological inquiry, so too are there many reasons to conduct research. Sometimes the reason to conduct research is simply to describe a social phenomenon. *Heat Wave*, published in 2003, is a study whose principal purpose is to describe the social characteristics of people who died in the infamous Chicago heat wave of 1995. Indicative of his descriptive purpose, the author Eric Klinenberg subtitled the study "A Social Autopsy of Disaster in Chicago." The study showed that important sociological factors related to heat-related mortality among Chicago's oldest residents included the desire of many to "age in place" while the surrounding environment changed; the idealization of personal independence among seniors and their consequent reluctance to ask for help; and differences between elderly men and women in the depth and breadth of their social networks.

Sometimes research is conducted to explain why something is occurring in society. Why do some marriages end in divorce? Why do some juveniles engage in delinquent behaviors? Why do some people succeed in life when others fail? "Why" is an essential question; in researching the answer, we develop and test theories that we then use to understand the social world. John H. Laub and Robert J. Sampson tackle such questions in their book *Shared Beginnings, Divergent Lives*. By studying a group of men, all of whom were juvenile delinquents, the authors learn why some of these men continued to be involved in crime throughout their lives and why others stopped. Attempting to answer "Why?" can have a profound impact on our understanding of the world.

Sometimes the goal of the research is to enact social change. Consider the role sociological research played in the desegregation of the K-12 school system in Florida. After the *Brown vs. the Board of Education of Topeka, Kansas* U.S. Supreme Court decision overturned segregation in the U.S. school system, Dick Ervin, Florida's attorney general at the time, was charged with desegregating Florida schools. He decided that in order to do this properly, he would call on sociologist Lewis Killian for assistance. Together they formed a bipartisan and biracial committee of sociologists, other social scientists, and educators to research the best way to desegregate the schools. The researchers looked at every school individually, determining what challenges were present at each and how to go about tackling those challenges. The result? Florida's schools never closed and desegregation was an overwhelmingly peaceful process. So why do research? Sometimes the answer is: To make the world a better place!

TYPES OF RESEARCH

Sociological research is generally divided into two main types: quantitative and qualitative. **Quantitative** research typically relies on statistics to make generalizations about subject matters of interest in studies of the social world. **Qualitative** research, on the other hand, is concerned with contextual data. The goal here is usually to produce a deep understanding of a social phenomenon. Many different quantitative and qualitative methods are discussed in depth in the following chapters. Aspects of quantitative and qualitative methods are often integrated into a single research study, known as a **multimethod** approach. They should not be viewed as oppositional methodologies.

Research, be it quantitative or qualitative, can take many forms. But there is a basic structure that most sociologists follow when conducting research and a basic research design that guides the research process, both of which are discussed in depth in this volume. We should begin by clarifying the two logical models that guide the overall research process whether it relies on a quantitative or qualitative approach: induction and deduction. In **inductive** research, the researcher begins with observations and then builds on these observations by collecting data. The data are eventually analyzed, and this analysis can lead to the development of a theory that explains what has been observed. The researcher does not go into the study with a set of questions to answer. Instead, what is initially observed guides the process.

Inductive research is based on observations. A researcher may notice while observing people at a homeless shelter that there are several single fathers with children. This is not something the researcher has seen before so more observation is done. The researcher may, at some point, decide to conduct interviews with these fathers and some members of the shelter's staff to explore what has been observed. Through the interviews the researcher learns how these fathers became homeless and what it is like for them to be single, homeless fathers. In the end, a theory may be developed to explain how fathers become homeless or why there is an increase in the number of single homeless fathers.

Deductive research, on the other hand, begins with a theory about some social phenomenon that leads to the development of a research question or **hypothesis** to be tested through data that are then collected and analyzed. A hypothesis is a stated prediction about the relationship between variables of interest in a research study. In deductive research, theory generates hypotheses; hypotheses point to certain kinds of data required to test them; data are analyzed to determine whether they support a hypothesis or not. Although there are exceptions, qualitative methods typically rely more on induction while quantitative research relies more on deduction.

THEORY AND RESEARCH

While theory is discussed in depth in another volume, it is important to provide in this volume at least an overview of what theory is and its role in sociological research. A **theory** is an explanation of some observed phenomenon. The explanation is a result of thorough observation and analysis of data. Method and theory are related and dependent on one another in research. Data are collected and analyses are conducted in order to develop theories in inductive work. Deductive work often involves testing theories that have been developed over time. Theory is essential even in descriptive research. For example, suppose you have become interested in homelessness and want to conduct a survey of homeless people in a local shelter. What questions will you ask? You might include questions about prior treatment for alcohol and drug disorders, but only because you have some sort of theory that says that addiction might lead to homelessness. You probably would not ask a question about whether your subjects were left- and right-handed. And why not? Because you cannot think of any theoretical reason why being right- or left-handed would be linked to homelessness. The key is relevance. So even crafting a survey questionnaire requires theorizing about factors that are and are not relevant to the subject at hand.

Oftentimes theories will be developed using both inductive and deductive methods. One example is the theory of "stereotype threat." This theory posits that members of minority groups often underperform because they are fearful of living up to a negative stereotype. The theory was initially formulated by social psychologist Claude Steele and his colleagues, who noticed that some minority students at the university where Steele taught were not performing at the same level as nonminority students. (It was this initial observation that got him thinking of possible reasons or theories, which makes the process inductive). Steele rejected the idea that minority students were not as capable as the other students and began seeking sociological explanations, eventually coming up with the stereotype threat theory. He then set out to test this theory (using deduction) and discovered, through his research, that his theory was in fact supported. This theory is currently being tested by others and is being applied to areas other than academic achievement, including parenting ability and even driving ability. Others therefore continue to test this theory using deductive methods.

The reciprocal relationship between theory and research has been widely discussed. C. Wright Mills stated that the "The primary purpose of both [method and theory] is clarity of conception and economy of procedure, and most importantly, the release rather than the restriction of the sociological imagination." Method and theory work together to allow the sociological imagination to be put to full use. Robert K. Merton, a prominent 20th century sociologist, explained that "empirical research goes far beyond the passive role of verifying and testing theory; it does more than confirm or refute hypotheses. Research plays an active role: it performs at least four major functions which help shape the development of theory. It initiates, it reformulates, it deflects, and it clarifies theory." Thus the relationship is reciprocal and ongoing in sociological research studies.

TYPES OF RESEARCH STUDIES

There are four main types of research studies. The first is **descriptive**. This is research that describes a social phenomenon and typically comprises the first studies done on a particular topic of interest. It is important to accurately describe a social phenomenon before moving on to other types of studies. Let's take the case of initial research into the phenomenon of covenant marriage (see Sidebar below for an explanation on covenant marriage). Most people had never heard of covenant marriage so initial research described what it is, what types of people were selecting covenant marriages, and how prevalent it was. Descriptive studies can be thought of as studies that answer the basic questions of who, what, when, and where.

The second common type of research study is **exploratory**. This type of study focuses on meaning. Once a phenomenon has been described, reasons and motivations for the behavior can be explored. The purpose is to build on descriptive work, but the study extends the research by delving deeper into the reasons that the phenomenon of interest exists and sometimes answers the question "why?" Continuing with our example, exploratory research via in-depth interviews examined two questions—why couples were motivated to enter into covenant marriages and what they understand their respective obligations to be within this marital option.

The third type of research study is **explanatory**. This type of study, as the name implies, focuses on explaining why a phenomenon is the way it is. The research focuses on possible causal relationships, or cause and effect. It answers

In covenant marriages, couples undergo premarital counseling and give up their right to a no-fault divorce. *(Shutterstock)*

Covenant Marriage

In the book, *Covenant Marriage: The Movement to Reclaim Tradition in America*, sociologists Steven Nock, Laura Sanchez, and James D. Wright discuss their study of this relatively new social phenomenon. Covenant marriage is a type of marriage that couples obtaining a marriage license can select. It differs from traditional marriage in two key ways: 1) couples selecting a covenant marriage must undergo premarital counseling, and 2) couples that select a covenant marriage must give up their right to a no-fault divorce. At the time of this study covenant marriage was an option in only three states: Louisiana, Arizona, and Arkansas. The study, which was conducted from 1999–2004, employed various research methods (including surveys, interviews, and experiments) to examine covenant marriage in the state of Louisiana.

the question "how?" The explanatory study focusing on covenant marriage consisted of an analysis of divorce rates among couples who opted for a covenant marriage compared to couples who opted for a traditional marriage.

The fourth basic type of social research is **evaluation**. Evaluation research focuses on evaluating the effectiveness of programs and policies. This is a special type of research that can involve a variety of methods and is a way that researchers can apply their skills outside of academia. With regards to covenant marriage, the research evaluated how the law was being interpreted in the various parishes in the state of Louisiana where couples can opt for covenant marriage, and how the marriage clerks were presenting the covenant marriage option to couples soliciting marriage licenses. All of the information could then be used to improve the program.

Oftentimes, as in the case of the covenant marriage study, several types of studies will be a part of one larger research project. However, these studies can also be done individually. Researchers build on the works of others. Therefore one researcher may conduct a descriptive study while other researchers may design studies that are exploratory, explanatory, or evaluative.

Cross-sectional and Longitudinal Studies

Studies of all four basic types described above can also be either cross-sectional or longitudinal. **Cross-sectional** research is research that takes place at one point in time. The majority of research studies are cross-sectional because this method is typically less expensive and quicker than conducting longitudinal research. Although the research study may take a long time, it is cross-sectional if all of the data are collected at one point in time. So if you decide to distribute a survey to 1,000 people, even though this may take weeks, the research would be cross-sectional. People that participate in the survey are not contacted at a later date and asked to participate again in the research study to examine how (or whether) their views or experiences may have changed.

Longitudinal studies are done over time or in waves. Data are collected at different times to assess changes in thoughts, perceptions, attitudes, or behaviors. Longitudinal studies are more time intensive and expensive than cross-sectional studies, but they can provide researchers with invaluable data regarding causality, or cause and effect.

Types of Longitudinal Studies

There are several types of longitudinal studies. One type is called a **trend study**. A trend study focuses on a specific topic and asks the same or very similar questions over time. The sample will be composed of different people in each study, but the topic remains unchanged. Political polls are an example of a trend study. During elections season, polls are taken frequently to assess voters' preferences. Results from these types of polls can show candidates where they are gaining or losing support. If a candidate finds from a poll that he is losing ground with a key demographic, say married women, the candidate can take measures to campaign actively to that particular group.

Political polls are conducted in a relatively short time span. Some trend studies take place over a much longer span of time. For example, a survey could be conducted annually of residents in a community to assess their satisfaction with city services, their use of parks and other public areas, and their opinions on what they think the best things about the community are. The data could be used to help community leaders make decisions about how the community's resources should be distributed.

A **cohort study** is another type of longitudinal research. Here the focus is on a specific population or cohort. Although the people surveyed in each sample may be different, they are all members of the same cohort, or members of the same generation. Examples of cohorts are Baby Boomers or members of Generation X. Another example of a cohort is a group of people that enter an academic institution in the same grade at the same time. So entering freshmen in a high school would be a cohort until they graduated four years later. The purpose of cohort studies is to assess changes in attitudes or beliefs over time. Researchers have conducted many cohort studies on members of the baby-boom generation, focusing on topics such as attitudes toward abortion and legalization of marijuana, use of various technologies, and volunteerism.

Panel studies, another type of longitudinal research, differ from trend and cohort studies in that the same people participate in every data collection episode. The participants may be asked different questions during data collection times or may even be asked about entirely different topics. Although the questions and topics may change, the people participating remain the same. One key benefit to this type of study is that researchers can assess which groups' opinions, beliefs, or attitudes have changed and for what reasons.

The Panel Study of Income Dynamics (PSID), begun in 1968, is an excellent example of a panel survey. It is a longitudinal study of a representative sample of U.S. individuals (men, women, and children) and their corresponding family units. The survey has focused on the dynamic aspects of economic and demographic behavior, that is, on annual fluctuations that determine whether a household is above or below the poverty line and the changing economic and demographic factors that influence a family's economic situation. Through the PSID, we have learned, for example, that while only 10–15 percent of all families are below poverty in any given year, over the span of a decade, as many as one family in three will experience at least one episode of poverty. Starting with a sample of 4,800 U.S. families in 1968, the sample size has grown to more than 7,500 families. In fact, at the conclusion of the 2003 data collection, the PSID will have collected information about more than 65,000 individuals, spanning as much as 36 years of their lives.

SUMMARY

Sociologists conduct research on many different topics. Many sociologists study the macrostructures that organize and characterize a society, such as race, ethnicity, class, or gender. Other sociologists study society's institutions: the family, the educational system, the world of work. Still others conduct research on social processes and change, for example, how parents socialize children and how parental values for children have evolved over time. Many sociologists focus on social problems, including crime and the justice system, poverty and homelessness, and the like. And some do research on microprocesses, such as interpersonal interactions. The methods used to study these topics can be quite diverse, ranging from survey research methods and quantitative analysis to ethnographic and other qualitative methods, such as focused interviews and group discussions. The following chapters will explore the different methods that sociologists use to conduct research.

Further Reading

Conley, Dalton. *Honky*. New York: Vintage Books, 2001.
Klinenberg, Eric. *Heat Wave: A Social Autopsy of Disaster in Chicago*. Chicago: The University of Chicago Press, 2002.
Merton, Robert King. *Social Theory and Social Structure*. New York: Free Press, 1968.

Mills, C. Wright. *The Sociological Imagination.* Oxford, England: Oxford University Press, 1968.

Weber, Max, Hans Heinrich Gerth (translator), and C. Wright Mills (translator). From *Max Weber: Essays in Sociology.* New York: Oxford University Press, 1958.

CHAPTER 2

QUANTITATIVE METHODS

British philosopher Alfred North Whitehead wrote in *The Aims of Education* that "the world is infected with quantity. To talk sense, is to talk in quantities. It is no use saying that the nation is large—How large? It is no use saying that radium is scarce—How scarce? You cannot evade quantity." Being able to quantify helps us make sense of the social world. We want to know quantities and the relationships among them: how much, how many, how often. Quantities are not the end of understanding, but they can be the beginning.

Quantitative methods allow social researchers to systematically quantify the world in which we live. Common quantitative methods include conducting experiments and administering surveys. Unobtrusive measures are also used often in quantitative research and commonly include conducting content analyses or analyzing artifacts such as graffiti writings or case records.

EXPERIMENTS

Experiments are viewed as the ideal method in most scientific research. This is because a true experiment, when done properly, can test hypotheses in a pure environment free from outside influences. However, because sociological research very rarely takes place in a laboratory, true experiments are not common. Nonetheless they are important to know about because quasi-experimental designs, which are research designs similar to true experiments, are quite common in sociology but can only be fully appreciated when compared to the experimental ideal.

The basic design of a true experiment is quite simple. First you need two groups: a treatment group and a control group. The treatment group is the group that will receive the **intervention**, or manipulation of the variable of interest. The control group will not.

Members of the two groups (control and treatment) must be randomly assigned. That is, the researcher does not make decisions about who will go into each group; group assignment is the result of some random process. Because individuals participating in the study are randomly assigned, potential bias will be avoided because both groups are more likely to be equally matched except for random differences. Both groups need to be administered a pretest and a posttest. A pretest is administered before the experiment to collect baseline data. A posttest is administered after the intervention is complete. Then the results between the pre- and posttests can be compared to determine if the treatment has produced a significant difference. That is, did the treatment group change significantly compared to the control group on the outcome of interest?

Let's take a simple example to explain the process more fully. Suppose a researcher wanted to test the efficacy of an intensive math training session on test performance. To do this she could work with a classroom of students, giving each student a number. Numbers would then be drawn out of a hat to separate students randomly, with half going to the control group and the other half to the treatment group. All participants would take a pretest to assess their mathematical abilities. The treatment group would then go through a four-hour math seminar. The control group would not have any special math training during this time. At the end of the four hours both groups would take a posttest. Then the researcher would compare the results. If the control group scored significantly higher on the posttest as compared to the control group, the researcher would conclude that the math seminar was successful.

Of course when experiments are being conducted there are many other factors that must be taken into account, many of which will be discussed below. But it is even more important to note that this type of design rarely fits with topics that sociologists study. Before even considering an experimental design, you need to ask the following questions:

- Is it possible to precisely categorize the people, places, or things in your study?
- Is it possible to select random people, places, or things in your study?
- Is the process of random placement of individuals into experimental and control groups ethical and legal?

In most cases, the second and third of these three questions often preclude true experimental designs in sociology. You can get away with experiments in other social sciences, like education and psychology, if you're experimenting with relatively harmless educational techniques or some simple perception or memory test, or if the control condition is what subjects would receive whether an experiment was being conducted or not. However, the subjects sociologists often use in their studies are defendants, prisoners, homeless people, or agency personnel. This could pose situations where it would either be unethical or illegal to benefit one group with an experimental treatment while depriving another group (the control group) of the same treatment. In general, if there's any risk of harm from delivering or withholding services to anybody in your sample, you cannot use an experimental design.

Some experiments are called **blind experiments**, which mean that you have gone out of your way to make sure the subjects don't know which group they're in, the experimental or control group. The term **double-blind experiment** means that the subjects and the researchers do not even know who is in which group. The double-blind experiment helps prevent researchers from inadvertently treating subjects differently or adding any sort of bias to the experiment. These precautions also help protect your study from the **Hawthorne Effect,** the tendency of subjects to act differently when they know they are being studied, especially if they think they have been singled out from some experimental treatment. The Hawthorne Effect is a phenomenon documented in 1950 by Henry Landsberger during his analysis of experiments conducted in the 1920s at the Hawthorne Works factory. These experiments consisted of researchers manipulating the workplace environment by doing things such as increasing the level of light in the factory, relocating work stations, increasing the length of break times and so forth. In nearly all situations, Landsberger noted, it seemed that the workers' productivity increased. It was discovered, however, that productivity did not increase because of these interventions, but rather because the workers knew that they were being watched.

The Hawthorne Effect has been widely challenged on many levels, and these challenges include questions about the scientific rigor of the original experiments (for example there was no control group in place), the original analysis of the data, and the conclusions that were drawn. But regardless of the debates on the way the Hawthorne Effect was first exposed, the fact remains that people can and do alter their behavior when they know they are being watched. Because sociologists want to get at the truth and see how people genuinely react to intervention(s), efforts must be made to prevent the Hawthorne Effect from impacting the results. For this reason, many researchers try to be as unobtrusive as possible.

QUASI-EXPERIMENTS

Oftentimes in sociological research a true experiment is not possible but a **quasi-experimental design** is. A quasi-experiment is similar to a true experiment in that a treatment group and a comparison group are compared. It differs from an experiment because participants are not randomly assigned to the two groups. Instead, participants are assigned to one group or the other.

For example, a researcher interested in examining the effectiveness of a tutoring program on improving grade point averages might choose to do a quasi-experiment. Let's suppose that the school has 1,000 students and that 100 of these students have participated in the tutoring program. To determine whether the program is effective the researcher conducts a quasi-experiment. The first step is to obtain a list of the 900 student that did not participate and a list of the 100 that did. GPAs for all 1,000 students from the beginning of the semester are also collected. Control group participants can be "matched" to treatment group members. Matching ensures that treatment and control group members are the same or similar in certain specified ways. The researcher in this study will match students based on their entering GPA. So if a person in the treatment group has an entering GPA of 3.6, a control group member will also have an entering GPA of 3.6. The researcher could also decide to match participants on other characteristics, such as gender or race.

For this example we will assume the researcher matched only on the basis of GPA. To pull the members of the control group, the list of the 900 nonparticipating students is sorted by GPA. One hundred of the nonparticipating students are selected through a process called sampling (this will be discussed in depth in Chapter 7).

At this point, the quasi-experiment would proceed as if it were a true experiment. After the tutoring program was complete the researcher would obtain the GPAs for the 100 participants and for the 100 students in the control group. Their post-program GPAs would be compared to determine if the students in the treatment group had significantly higher GPAs than the students in the control group.

Although quasi-experiments do not boast the rigorous design that true experiments do, they are typically more appropriate for sociological research and can be conducted in a systematic way. They can be a very effective method for determining the impact of a particular intervention. Quasi-experiments can even determine the impact that watching a certain television program or movie can have on people's perceptions of a particular issue.

SURVEY RESEARCH

While experiments and quasi-experiments are important in sociological research, a much more commonly used quantitative method is surveying. Surveys in fact have been the most common way to collect quantitative sociological data for decades. They allow for data to be collected on virtually any topic and produce generalizable results. By "generalizable" we mean that the results of a properly done survey can be applied to others in the population of interest. There are five main ways, or **modes**, that surveys can be administered: via mail, telephone, or Internet, in person, and group administered. There are advantages and disadvantages to all five types of survey modes, and the ideal mode for a particular study will be determined by a number of factors, including the topic being researched and the resources available to the researchers.

Survey Research Concerns
In all modes of survey research, a concern for researchers is the degree to which the responses given by respondents reflect what the respondents truly think and believe. Do the answers reflect reality? In connection with this, a major concern in survey research is **social desirability**—a phenomenon that occurs when respondents give answers that are socially acceptable instead of answers that are honest. Questions regarding racist or sexist beliefs or attitudes toward homosexuals can fall victim to social desirability. So can rather innocuous questions such as: Did you vote in the last election? Or are you satisfied with your job? Studies that have compared the percentages of people in a community that say they voted and actual numbers of people who voted in the same community find that many more people say they voted than actually voted. Why? Voting is a socially desirable behavior and many respondents want to be perceived positively, even by researchers they don't know personally.

Another concern with the answers given by respondents in survey research is **response set tendencies**. Response set tendencies refer to ways in which respondents tend to answer questions regardless of the question content. An example of how this works illustrates the phenomenon. Suppose, for example, that people are being asked a list of ten questions that all have the answer options: strongly agree, agree, disagree, and strongly disagree. A response set tendency would be a respondent selecting only "strongly agree" or "strongly disagree" (the extreme options). Another example is respondents always selecting "yes" in yes/no questions. There are measures that can be put in place to catch these sorts of biases. However, preventing them, which is greatly preferred, is much more challenging.

Achieving high response rates is another concern researchers have when conducting surveys. The **response rate** is a calculation of the number of people that complete a survey divided by the number of people to which the survey was sent. So if a survey is sent to 1,000 people and 600 complete it, then the response rate is .60 or 60 percent. The higher the response rate, the better. If the response rate is very low, we worry about how accurately our findings will generalize to the larger population. If out of 1,000 people only 75 return the survey, the response rate will be so low that the generalizability of the survey results can be jeopardized. There are many ways to increase response rates for each type of survey. A common way is by using **incentives**, which are inducements to encourage people to participate in research (for example, a $10 gift card).

Mail

One way that surveys can be administered is by mail. This involves developing a list of questions that a respondent can answer personally (i.e., without verbal prompts or instructions from a researcher) and is called a **self-administered questionnaire**. Mail surveys are not used as frequently as they once were, but they are still a valuable way to collect data. The U.S. Census Bureau uses a mail survey as its primary method of data collection as do many marketing firms conducting marketing research. A recent sociological research project that relied on mail surveys examined community residents' level of social capital (that is, how connected people are to others and to their community).

There are many advantages associated with this mode of surveying. First, compared to some of the other survey modes, it is relatively inexpensive. The only real costs of data collection are postage and printing of survey materials; follow-ups and incentives will, of course, increase costs. Second, it is possible to solicit input from a large number of people. Literally thousands of survey questionnaires can be distributed in a single day via mail. Third, participants have the freedom to complete the surveys at their convenience, when and where they like. This option alone may make people more inclined to complete the questionnaire. Fourth, mail surveys can accommodate a lot of questions (including relatively long questions that might not be acceptable to people responding to survey questionnaires in other modes) because people who are taking the survey at their convenience and in the comfort of their own home are more likely to answer them. Finally, because a researcher is not the one asking the questions directly, people may feel more comfortable answering the questions honestly. This allows the researcher to ask questions that people may not feel comfortable answering in person or on the phone.

As with every mode of surveying, mail surveys have some disadvantages. Although there is a concern about response rate with all survey modes, mail surveys can have particularly low response rates. One obvious reason for this is that potential respondents can easily discard the material, often without even reading it. Because of the volume of mail that many households receive (a lot of it being "junk" mail), there is always the possibility that your survey will be thrown out.

A second disadvantage to this mode is that if a participant decides to fill out the questionnaire but has questions, there is no one to provide answers. If a participant is confused or uncertain, he or she may simply skip the question or may answer it in a way that does not actually answer the question as the researcher intended it. Third, understanding what people have written can be a challenge for researchers when it comes time to enter the data. Respondents' handwriting can be difficult to read, they may circle three answer options when the directions call for selecting one, or they may skip entire pages of the questionnaire. All of this can result in poor-quality data. A related issue is that the data typically need to be entered into a computer program for analysis. Unlike other modes where the data are entered into the program while it is being collected, this mode requires people to enter the data after it has been collected. The data entry process can introduce error (for example, someone may accidentally key in an incorrect response).

While mail surveys are not as popular as they once were, they are still a viable option for survey research. This is particularly true if you want to contact a lot of people in a relatively short amount of time across a vast geographical area.

Telephone

In the United States, telephone surveys have been the primary mode of survey data collection for nearly sixty years. The universal availability of telephone service, efficient sampling techniques and **Computer Assisted Telephone Interviewing** (CATI) systems, all make telephone data collection easier. CATI systems allow telephone surveyors to read questions from a computer screen and enter respondents' answers into a data collection program, eliminating the need for after-the-fact data entry.

One major concern about telephone surveys is the quality of the sample being called. It is estimated that approximately 30 percent of telephone numbers are unlisted. More importantly, households with unlisted numbers differ in important ways from those with listed numbers. Namely (and perhaps surprisingly), people with unlisted numbers often have low incomes. Another major concern with telephone surveys is the increasing number of people that have no landline telephone.

It is common knowledge among those conducting telephone surveys that response rates to this survey mode continue to decline. Many people do not want to speak to solicitors of any kind by telephone. Technology, like answering machines and caller ID and other innovations, ensure that people have the option of answering a phone only when they know who is calling them and if they wish to speak with whoever it is that is calling. And it certainly seems that most people find screening calls a very desirable feature of phone service because it has become more difficult for survey researchers to contact respondents via telephone.

The prevalence of identity theft is certainly not helping this situation. Some of the questions that sociologists might want to ask may make potential respondents very uncomfortable. Consider a telephone survey done by the University of Central Florida's Institute for Social and Behavioral Sciences, which was examining the impact of being a member of "the working poor," that is, people who work but are in or near poverty. The very first question in the survey asked respondents what their annual income was the previous year. It was essential to get this answer first to determine if the respondent was in fact considered to be "low income." Convincing people that the study was ethical, the responses were confidential, and that no individual's answers would be made publicly available was quite a challenge. Many potential respondents refused to continue participating after this initial question was asked. The issue of bias against telephone surveys has been extensively researched, and surveyors are actively trying to find methods to combat reluctance on the part of potential respondents to participate.

Despite these concerns, telephone surveys are still widely used. To begin with, they are relatively inexpensive (particularly when compared to in-person interviews). Second, CATI systems (computer programs that telephone surveyors use to administer a survey) provide a high amount of control over the administration of questionnaires because, as noted above, they ensure that data entry occurs as the telephone survey is in progress, not later. CATI systems also make skip logic very simple. **Skip logic** is a component of surveys that direct respondents to skip or answer different question options, depending on how they answer a particular question in previous a section or sections of the survey. Telephone surveys can also be used to explore a wide range of topics. They provide a level of comfort because the surveyor and the respondent are not face to face. However, because the surveyor and respondent are communicating in "real time," it is possible to clarify information and probe for additional details.

Example of skip logic

1. Do you have a pet?
2. Do you have a cat?

    a. How many cats do you have?
    b. Indoor or outdoor?
    c. How old?

3. Do you have a dog?

    a. How many dogs do you have?
    b. What is/are the breed of the dog(s)?
    c. How old?

A respondent saying "no" to question number 1, would not be asked questions 2 and 3. If someone answered "yes" to number 1, the survey would go on to question number 2. If the answer to number 2 was "no," questions 2a, 2b, and 2c would be skipped. As you can imagine skip logic can get very complicated, but CATI systems make it a simple process. Because skip logic is programmed into the system, only respondent-relevant questions come up on the screen for the surveyor to ask.

Internet

The fastest growing way to conduct surveys is on the Internet. But although Internet surveys have become a very popular data collection method in recent years, they are not always a suitable option. They work best when there is a list of the population of interest and when the population of interest has full Internet access. For example, an online survey can be a great way to survey college students at a university. Most universities provide students with email addresses, and students typically have access to computers.

Internet surveys are becoming popular for several reasons. First, a large amount of data can be collected from a lot people very quickly. An email with a link to a survey can be sent out in an email "blast" to hundreds of people simultaneously. This is not only efficient but also inexpensive. There are many online survey questionnaire programs that are free or charge a very low monthly fee. Moreover, access to a suitable survey program may be the only cost incurred by a research team using online surveying. In addition, Internet surveys have the potential to ensure anonymity to respondents. Because there is no interaction with a surveyor, topics can be quite sensitive. In some cases Internet surveys may provide access to unique populations, such as those who are members of online dating sites, those who are members of virtual communities, or those who engage in deviant behavior. From a researcher's perspective (and this particularly applies to unfunded researchers), one of the best things about Internet surveys is that there is no data entry. The survey respondents do the data entry for you!

There are, however, some basic limitations, which include matters related to Internet access and the response rate. There has been a rapid rise in the proportion of U.S. households that have access to the Internet, but just because a person has access to the Internet does not mean that the person can actually be contacted through this mode. Further, there is no central list of households or persons with Internet access, and it may be nearly impossible to create such a list. It has been suggested that the difference between those people with access to the Internet and those without are significant, especially with respect to demographics such as income, education, race/ethnicity, and age. This alone may make researchers hesitant to generalize findings to a large population.

As with all types of surveys, response rate is a key concern. Typically, online surveys have a lower response rate when compared to other types of survey modes. It is extremely easy for someone who gets an email about a survey to hit the delete button. Sociologists using this mode often have to send several reminder emails to achieve the desired response rate. Although it takes very little effort to send out an initial email announcing the survey, it takes much more effort to remind people that participating in the survey is important.

Internet surveys are easy to design (although writing good questions takes time), they can be sent to a large population very quickly, and require no data entry by surveyors. The ease in distributing surveys on the Internet has led to many people who are not researchers to launch their own surveys. Companies, for example, send out surveys to their employees to get feedback on any number of issues. Companies can also solicit opinions regarding their products or services from their customers. You have no doubt been online and had a pop-up announce: "We want to hear from you!" The sheer volume of survey requests can lead to a lower response rate for researchers conducting surveys for scientific purposes, simply because people suffer from **survey fatigue**. Potential respondents receive so many requests to participate in surveys that they are not willing to participate.

Negatives aside, by nearly all accounts Internet surveying will continue to grow. Research is now focusing on how to increase response rates and how to conduct Internet surveys that are representative of a large population. One promising strategy is to use telephone samples to generate lists of willing respondents with email addresses, computer access, and a predetermined interest in participating in online surveys. Continued research in how to make Internet surveys more representative will surely make them even more popular in the future.

In Person

In-person, or face-to-face, surveys consist of an interviewer asking a participant a series of questions. The interviewer uses a questionnaire to ensure that all participants are asked the same questions, in the same order. Face-to-face surveys have a distinct advantage over other types of surveys. To begin with, the interviewer is the one filling out the questionnaire, ensuring accurate data entry. (On the other hand, in-person surveys can be considerably longer than surveys that require the participant to fill out the survey form. Some in-person surveys take as long as an hour or more.) A second advantage is that the interviewer can probe for information. A **probe** is a follow-up question designed to elicit more information from a participant. Third, because the interviewer is filling out the actual questionnaire, errors resulting from respondents not clearly indicating their responses can be avoided.

While this mode has many benefits, in-person interviewing can be very expensive to conduct. Consider the study that involved in-person surveying that was conducted by Jana Jasinski and her colleagues in their exploration of levels of violence experienced among women residing in homeless shelters. Case managers at five homeless shelters in five cities in Florida were paid to administer a total of 800 surveys. All participants were paid for their time (as the surveys took about an hour to an hour and a half to conduct). Once all of the data were collected, data entry personnel were paid to enter the data. A

Advantage and Disadvantages of Survey Modes

Mode	Advantages	Disadvantages
Mail	Relatively inexpensive Send a lot of questionnaires at oncez Cover large geographic area	Low response rate Respondents can't clarify questions Lots of data entry
Telephone	Collect a lot of data relatively quickly No data entry Interviewers can clarify questions	Can be expensive Difficult to find willing participants Social desirability issues
Online	Send a lot of questionnaires at once No data entry	Low response rate Need email addresses of sample
In Person	Can use long questionnaires Ability to probe	Can be costly Takes a long time to collect data Lots of data entry
Group Administered	Relatively inexpensive Collect a lot of data quickly Researcher is there during data collection	Needs institutional setting Lots of data entry Questionnaire should be short

related issue is that because the questionnaires are often lengthy, it can take a relatively long time to collect data. In the case in question, data collection took more than a year. A third concern is related to the potential bias that can be introduced when using this mode. If researchers conducting in-person interviews are not careful to administer the interviews the same way for all of the participants, bias can become a significant concern. You want the participants to have as similar an experience as possible to minimize bias. This can be difficult, particularly when many different people are administering the surveys.

You may think that a major concern would be the type of topics that could be discussed using this mode and that sensitive topics would need to be avoided, but this is often not the case. In Jasinski et al.'s research, participants were asked in great detail about their past experiences with violence. A related concern, however, is how honestly participants are answering the questions. Women in a homeless shelter may have legitimate reasons for not wanting to disclose all of their past (or current) experiences, particularly if these admissions would show them to be in violation of shelter rules. However, by establishing rapport with the participants and ensuring confidentiality, sensitive topics can be properly studied.

In-person surveys, while expensive and time consuming, can generate immense amounts of rich and meaningful data. Because in-person surveys can be much longer and more time consuming than surveys conducted by other modes, the personal experiences as well as the opinions and beliefs that participants hold can be explored in depth.

Group Administered

Group-administered surveys are a less common mode of survey data collection. They are typically done in an institutional setting such as a university classroom or a workplace. In this mode, the researcher (or an assistant) distributes surveys to participants and the participants complete them on the spot. There are several benefits to this type of survey. First, the researcher can acquire a large sample in a short amount of time. Participants are in a central location, and thus the time spent on finding and recruiting participants is lessened significantly. Second, because the researcher is typically in the room while the surveys are being filled out, participants can ask questions about anything they may be confused about, which could lead to higher data quality. Third, again because the researcher is usually in the room, participation rates are very high. Because participants see the researcher, rather than being contacted by an anonymous caller or getting an unsolicited survey by mail, higher participation is more or less guaranteed. Fourth, this mode can be very convenient. For sociologists working at a university, collecting survey data from students can involve simply asking a colleague for permission to distribute surveys at the beginning or end of a class session. Arguably the most positive aspect of this method is that a large amount of data can be collected in an extremely short amount of time. It is very efficient and relatively inexpensive.

As with all survey methods, there are also some disadvantages. Given that group-administered surveys work best in institutional settings, the groups of people that can be in the sample are limited. Typically the respondents in this type of survey are college students or, to a lesser extent, employees in a particular company. Moreover, because the surveys are usually administered in classrooms on college campuses, the proximity of students to one another may prevent participants from answering questions honestly. If a survey is asking about people's drug use, criminal behaviors, or other sensitive topics, participants may conceal the truth for fear that other students may see their responses. Additionally, group-administered surveys cannot be very long. Because they are most often conducted in an institutional setting, there are other things that must be dealt with (such as class work!) so that taking an hour to do a survey is usually not practical.

Having the researcher present during data collection can also pose its own problems. Participants may feel pressured to take the survey even when they really do not want to. This is one reason researchers typically avoid surveying their own students. But even if respondents do not feel pressured, they may be disinterested. This can lead to respondents not reading questions carefully, or not answering the questions fully. Finally, as noted above, a lot of data are generated in a short amount of time, which is a good thing, except that once all those surveys are filled out someone has to enter them into a computer program for analysis. Although data-collection time is relatively short, data-processing time can be quite long depending on the length of the survey and the number of participants.

Group-administered surveys certainly have their place in social research, and there are times when they can be the best choice for researchers. This is particularly true when a sociologist who works at a university wants to conduct a study examining the perceptions, attitudes, or opinions of college students. The surveys can also be a great way for student researchers to learn the process of data collection. And self-administered student surveys can sometimes be useful as pretests or pilot studies for larger projects.

Mixed-Mode Surveys

Many researchers use more than one survey mode in a single research study. This allows researchers to give respondents a choice in the survey type with which they feel most comfortable. The result can often be higher response rates, less data collection time, and less overall cost. One such project which used multimodes was surveying high school seniors that had been accepted to a particular university. The university wanted to know why some of the students had decided to attend the university while others had decided to go elsewhere. A complete list of the population was available. This list also included email addresses. Because of this and the age of the students, an Internet survey was launched.

Students who had decided to attend the university quickly completed the survey on the Internet. However, far fewer students in the group of those that decided to go elsewhere were participating. A telephone survey, using the same questionnaire, was implemented. Telephone surveyors called all of the students that had not participated via Internet. The result? The response rate nearly doubled. This mixed-more approach raises some concern, particularly that using different surveying methods could negatively affect data quality. Researchers might wonder, for example, whether students who responded to the phone survey answered as honestly as those who completed the survey on the Internet (or vice versa). For this reason, it is important to maintain consistency across modes to the greatest extent possible. Statistical analysis can even determine if the answers given via different modes differ in significant ways. In the example above, the differences were not significant. That is those who had accepted admission were similar whether they completed the survey online or on the telephone (the same finding applied to those who had declined admission at the university).

UNOBTRUSIVE MEASURES

Unobtrusive measures involve research methods that do not require interaction with respondents. Unobtrusive measures are sometimes called nonreactive measures because the interaction with the researcher does not cause them to change in any way. Nonreactive measures can consist of analyzing any products made by humans. We call these objects **social artifacts**. Examples of social artifacts include photographs, music videos, books, and works of art. By analyzing these products, better insight into the social world can be obtained.

Content Analysis

A **content analysis** is the systematic analysis of social artifacts. It is an unobtrusive, quantitative method that systematically assesses meanings in objects that people have made. Virtually any type of social artifact can be analyzed. Researchers have conducted content analyses of television shows, movies, song lyrics, music videos, speeches, book genres, and art, among other things. A content analysis can be an excellent way to learn more about the world. Because the social artifacts are nonreactive, many common concerns associated with doing research (like worrying if people are answering honestly) become irrelevant.

Archives of major newspapers are readily available online and are commonly used by researchers conducting content analyses. Diana Kendall, for example, conducted a content analysis to examine how social class is portrayed in American society. As a part of her study, Kendall searched the archives of *The New York Times* to obtain articles for her analysis. Once in the archive, Kendall searched by keywords that indicated class level including "working class," "elites," and "middle class." These keyword searches led her to articles that discussed class level or socioeconomic status. After much searching and compiling of articles, Kendall had a sample of articles to explore how class is portrayed in *The New York Times*. (In her study, Kendall also analyzed television programs.)

Through her analysis Kendall discovered how the media present the various socioeconomic classes in different ways. She found that the media "uses a shorthand code for the presumed values and lifestyles of the upper, middle, working, and poverty classes." In articles about the upper class, the focus is often on lifestyle and material possessions. Those in the lower economic classes, including homeless people, are often portrayed in negative, stereotypical ways. Kendall suggested that this portrayal in the media can influence the way people think about others in the different social classes, but it is important to recall that researchers cannot determine effects simply by studying artifacts.

Types of Content

While there are exceptions, a content analysis usually measures social artifacts on two levels of meaning: manifest and latent. **Manifest content** refers to the explicit meaning that exists in the artifacts. In content analyses of textual data, this would be the "dictionary definitions" of words. If analyzing images, the manifest content would refer to the image itself. In an advertisement, for example, this would include the product being sold, descriptions of the model(s) in the ad, and so forth. **Latent content** is more difficult to interpret. Latent content is meaning that is implied. To code for this the researcher must be thoroughly informed of the context of the artifacts that are being coded, be it colloquial vernacular or symbols in visual presentations. In coding music lyrics for references to violence, a researcher might ask, "Are there terms that imply violence without saying it directly?" In analyzing an advertisement, the researcher might ask, "Is the model positioned in an aggressive or passive way?" Although latent content is more difficult to code than manifest content, a systematic approach makes it possible.

Example of a Content Analysis

As an undergraduate student, Jillian Mitchell conducted a content analysis examining the portrayal of Native Americans in public education. Through this study, she explored how Native Americans are portrayed as part of history and in the present day. Twenty social studies textbooks currently being used in the Florida public school system were acquired, coded, and analyzed to determine common themes and teachings on the subject of Native Americans in relation to the ways other racial groups have been studied and portrayed throughout history. The analysis tracked how often different tribes were discussed, what the topic of the passages were, and at what points in history they received the most exposure.

Throughout the course of the study, certain factors common to the majority of the texts became evident. After a few books were coded, certain themes surfaced and the study took a different approach. Rather than simply dissecting Native American roles, emphasis was placed on how their treatment was justified throughout history and how the imagery visually portrayed individual Native Americans and Native American cultures or tribes. What the research uncovered was that Native Americans were seen as one mass of people rather than as a large group comprising separate cultures. They were often seen as obstacles to overcome or simply part of the natural environment, both of which needed to be destroyed or changed. The ultimate finding was that everything that did happen to different tribes in history was deemed for the common good and necessary for the development of modern American values.

Content analysis presents its own unique concerns. One of the most serious is the availability of the artifacts under study. For some content analyses it is relatively easy to access all of the elements in the population—say, for example, every episode of the TV show *Friends*. For other mediums it might not be, such as all of the photographs taken by a particular photographer. In this case, all of the photographs may not be accessible. Some may have been destroyed; others are not accessible to the public. Deposit or **survival bias** happens when some of the individual artifacts are more available than others in the entire population. How do you know, for example, if all of the artifacts of a particular population are accessible? Sometimes this can be quite easy (television shows for example are typically numbered and lists of all episodes are available); sometimes this cannot be known (who is to say how many photographs a photographer took or how many paintings an artist produced?). The older the artifacts of interest, the more this can be problematic because it may be harder to determine how many artifacts actually existed and even more difficult to locate all of them. When making conclusions about the artifacts, the conclusions can only generalize to those that are accessible, which is not always the entire population.

Another concern when conducting content analyses is that it can be challenging to make inferences regarding the effects or impact of social artifacts. For example, suppose a content analysis reveals that children's cartoons have gotten progressively more violent over the past decades. What does that mean in terms of impact? Are children who watch these shows more violent as a result? Such causal relationships cannot be established through a content analysis of artifacts. Conclusions can be drawn only about the artifacts themselves; resulting impacts must be explored through other methods. Finally, you cannot ask artifacts questions; you can only study the properties they present.

Sampling

Just as with other types of research, sampling is needed when conducting a content analysis. Random samples are sometimes possible, and should be used. To do a random sample, you first need to assemble a sampling frame of all of the elements from the population. A special concern in sampling for a content analysis is **haphazard sampling**, which is acquiring artifacts to study because they are easily accessible or available. Analyzing artifacts because they are readily available can quickly result in a biased sample and therefore biased results. For example, say you want to examine how women are portrayed in hip-hop songs. Making a list of all of the songs that you can readily recall would be a haphazard sample. Your knowledge of the songs is not systematic and could be biased toward artists you happen to enjoy. A better way would be to develop a sampling frame that included all of the hip-hop songs that made the Billboard Top 100 in a year, or even several years. This is certainly not the only option; there are many ways to develop sampling frames that are not haphazard and that lend themselves better to an unbiased analysis.

Coding

Because the data involved in a content analysis are not typically numeric, standard data analysis techniques are not appropriate. For a content analysis, researchers use a process called coding to make sense of the information. **Coding** is the way in which the information in the artifacts is quantified. Researchers determine what to code for before beginning the actual coding process. For example, let's say a researcher has heard that advertisements are featuring models that vary from the traditional white, tall, and thin models that have been prominently featured for so long. The researcher decides the best way to approach this study is to conduct a content analysis analyzing diversity of female models in advertisements that are in a particular popular women's magazine. To assess change over time, magazine issues that span several years are used. The researcher decides she wants to examine the models on two dimensions: body type and race. The dimensions that will be coded need to be clearly defined before content analysis begins.

So how will the race of the models be assessed? Clearly race can be difficult to determine from a photo. The researcher could decide to assess visually and code on a spectrum from light to dark skin. Or she might decide to code models as white or nonwhite. There is no correct answer. (The same concerns must be addressed for measuring body type as well, of course.) What is essential is that the decision is made before coding and that the coding scheme is valid. To keep track of what she is seeing in the artifacts, the researcher needs a **code sheet**, which is used to record the same information for each case being analyzed (in this case the race and body types of the models in the advertisements in the magazines that have been sampled). There are many computer programs available that can assist researchers in constructing and maintaining code sheets.

Now you may be thinking that this seems like a very subjective process. Or that a researcher can easily "read into" texts or images to see what she is looking for. One way to help ensure that this is not the case is to test for inter-coder reliability. **Inter-coder reliability** (ICR) involves having more than one person code the artifacts on the same dimensions and then comparing the results. This can be calculated statistically using a correlation analysis. A high ICR is a correlation close to 1; a low ICR is closer to 0.

Content analysis is a great technique for being able to research the social world by examining things that people have produced. This is important as we are often influenced by the objects around us, whether we are aware of it or not. This is particularly true with different forms of media. Content analysis allows for an objective assessment of these objects. The important thing to remember is that content analyses should be conducted in a rigorous way that produces reliable and accurate results. When done properly, they can provide interesting insights about objects in our society and about how those objects reflect that society.

Existing Data

Another common unobtrusive method used in sociological research is analysis of existing data. This is not to be confused with **secondary data analysis** (the analysis of data collected by someone else through surveys or other methods). The analysis of existing data usually involves statistical analysis as a means to quantify, opposed to coding textual or visual data, as is the case in a content analysis.

Existing data can take many forms. Examples include client records, government statistics such as those collected by the U.S. Census Bureau, standardized test results, and medical records. The analysis of existing data allows researchers to examine topics of interest without asking respondents questions directly (and thus remaining unobtrusive). These data were initially collected for a specific purpose, often an administrative purpose. The sociologist using these existing data at a later time is almost certainly analyzing them for a different reason. Existing data from multiple sources can also be analyzed in a single study. A researcher might want to conduct a study using data from the U.S. Census to assess the demographic make-up of certain cities and simultaneously use data from the National Vital Statistics System to assess teenage pregnancy rates.

Existing data analysis boasts many of the same advantages content analysis does because the method is unobtrusive and thus the data are not impacted by the researcher's involvement. Another advantage is that the data are often very accessible. Government agencies that collect statistics usually make data available online, allowing researchers to easily download relevant files. Another asset is that by using existing data, researchers can conduct longitudinal studies and assess trends over time without actually having to conduct new (and usually expensive) longitudinal studies.

A major disadvantage of this existing data analysis is that the researcher has no control over what information the existing data may include. In the analysis of client records for example, the researcher may wish that clients had been asked about certain specific things relevant to the study. There is no way to correct for this when using this method. Moreover, data files, even those from government sources, can be difficult to work with. They are often very large files, and there can be large gaps because of missing data. Combining existing data from several sources can be even more of a challenge.

Although the data can be unwieldy, the vast amount of information collected by others presents sociologists with the opportunity to conduct important research studies that could be impossible were it not for existing source materials. Collecting data on a national level is out of reach for most research-

Example of Research with Existing Data

Sociologist Meghan Harte was interested in studying state level standardized test scores as an indicator that the No Child Left Behind Act (NCLB), a federally mandated educational policy, was working as intended. To do this she analyzed test scores of third grade students in Orange County, Florida, from 2005 to 2010 to review progress as well as to examine the relation of test scores to demographic data. Harte collected test scores from existing public records from the Florida Department of Education. By law the department is responsible for developing, administering, scoring, and reporting on standardized tests.

Using existing records, Harte compiled 245 sets of mean reading and math scores for individual elementary schools as well as the demographics for race and gender. The number of students at each school collecting free or reduced lunch was also collected as a way to measure socioeconomic status. Demographics by individual were collected and rates were computed for the percentages by race, gender, and free lunch by school and year. Harte was then able to test whether progress was being made and whether school demographics were correlated with test scores.

The analysis conducted was in line with the national literature: Scores for third graders in Orange County, Florida, rose between 2005 and 2010. From Harte's analysis, it appears that NCLB is working, that students are learning better. But one limitation of using existing data is that we cannot necessarily know why something happened. Student achievement scores may have improved because of the new mandates for assessment and accountability, or they may have improved by a series of other variables, such as teachers "teaching to the test."

ers, but relevant data are often available online. While existing data certainly cannot answer all of the questions sociologists attempt to answer, it is an ideal method to answer some.

Historical Research

A final unobtrusive method that will be discussed here is **historical research**, which uses existing historical documents in an analysis of past events to inform current life. It is, in simple terms, a combination of history and sociology. Some historical research is **comparative**, meaning that two similar entities (such as counties or events) are compared to one another, with researchers looking for similarities and differences in processes and outcomes. The progression of time is an essential component in historical research as events are chronologically traced to understand what occurred and how this has an impact on society today. The same techniques used in content analysis, in terms of coding textual documents, are used here. The goal, however, differs. Instead of determining themes among certain social artifacts (such as books or music videos), historical research codes for an understanding of what occurred over time, how one event influenced the next, and what this means to society.

One of the most well-known sociologists to use this method was Charles Tilly, and one of Tilly's most persistent questions was how the modern nation-state came to be the predominant political entity in the world. What, he wondered, makes the large nation-state historically preferable or more advantageous than, say, the smaller city-states of the medieval era? To answer this question, Tilly examined political, social, and technological changes in Europe from the Middle Ages to modern times. His theory was that various military innovations (in particular, the invention of firearms and the subsequent ascendance of the mass army) made warfare an extremely expensive proposition, a tactic of conquest, domination, and defense that could only be effectively exploited by states with large amounts of capital and large populations. Larger states, in short, could afford to pay for military security and that favored their survival in a hostile political and military environment. Thus, large nation-states with large military budgets and vast armies quickly swallowed up and incorporated smaller city-states, duchies, principalities, and other medieval political entities. It was by such processes that Bavaria, Prussia, Alsace, Lorraine, Holstein, Saxony, Baden, and many other principalities were swallowed up through military conquest to become, ultimately, the German nation-state.

Historical research can be extremely challenging. The researcher must first locate the relevant material, which might include historical documents, written accounts, oral accounts if available, and so forth. There is often an immense amount of data that must be sorted through and organized. The materials may be spread out across many locations; some of the material may not be publicly accessible, and some may no longer exist. Once the materials are located and organized they must be verified, which means copious cross-checking before sources can be analyzed and findings can be interpreted.

SUMMARY

Many of the questions we want to ask about society and social relationships are fundamentally quantitative: How many people favor legalization of marijuana? How many pregnancies are terminated annually by abortion? Is the average age at first marriage is increasing or decreasing over time? Or perhaps we want to learn something about the strength of the relationship between education and income, or differences in self-esteem between boys and girls, or differences in life expectancy between blacks and whites. These and many thousands more questions demand quantitative answers and those answers in turn depend on methods that will produce quantitative data. It is senseless to talk about "many people" if you cannot say how many. And you cannot say how many without some method of counting. And although people sometimes object to be treated "like a number," often all we want or need to know about them can be expressed in measured quantities. As Dr. Samuel Johnson put it, "The good of counting is that it brings everything to a certainty, which before floated in the mind indefinitely." The quantitative researcher believes that certainty is always preferable!

Further Reading

Kendall, Diana Elizabeth. *Framing Class: Media Representations of Wealth and Poverty in America*. Lanham, Md.: Rowman & Littlefield Publishers, 2005.

Marsden, Peter V., and James D. Wright. *Handbook of Survey Research*. 2nd ed. Bingley, UK: Emerald, 2010.

Riffe, Daniel, Stephen Lacy, and Frederick Fico. *Analyzing Media Messages: Using Quantitative Content Analysis in Research*. 2nd ed. Mahwah, N.J.: Lawrence Erlbaum, 2005.

Tilly, Charles, and Lesley J. Wood. *Social movements, 1768–2008*. 2nd ed. Boulder, Colo.: Paradigm Publishers, 2009.

Webster, Murray, and Jane Sell. *Laboratory Experiments in the Social Sciences*. Amsterdam: Academic Press/Elsevier, 2007.

CHAPTER 3

QUALITATIVE METHODS

Qualitative methods differ from quantitative methods in that they focus on generating textual data, not numbers. Whereas quantitative research quantifies answers to questions like who, what, how many, and how often, qualitative research strives to get at the meanings behind the numbers. Qualitative methods explore the reasons and motivations for perceptions, beliefs, and behaviors of people and can produce a better understanding of the lived experiences of people. At a very basic level, qualitative methods primarily involve observing and talking to people. Because the data collected are textual and visual, not numeric, the way the data are analyzed differs as well. Qualitative data are typically coded and analyzed for themes or patterns.

Qualitative research is sometimes criticized for not being scientific or objective. It can, however, be both. It is true that qualitative studies do not produce *statistically* meaningful results and that the results of the studies typically do not generalize to a larger population of interest. But qualitative research can provide a deeper understanding of social phenomena. It can illuminate the social world in a way that quantitative research simply cannot. For example, while many studies have told us who is homeless and how people become homeless, qualitative works have taught us what it feels like to be homeless.

Oftentimes students assume that because qualitative research involves words and observations, it must be "easier" than quantitative research. This is not the case. Qualitative research often takes more time and generates much more data that must be analyzed than do quantitative studies. One method is not inherently superior to the other. They both have their strengths and their weaknesses. The research question should guide the researcher to the appropriate method for a particular study. When qualitative methods seem more appropriate, they should be used.

There are numerous examples of qualitative works in sociology that have provided us with a deep understanding of people and society in general. One example is *Tally's Corner: A Study of Negro Streetcorner Men* by Elliot Liebow. Based on 19 months of field observation, this book allows people to understand the lives of a group of people many had often driven past but never given much consideration. The study centers on a group of men that lived and congregated in a particular area in Washington, D.C. While casual observation may lead some people to assume that these men were just wasting time hanging on street corners, Liebow learned that there was in fact a lot more going on than was apparent.

Liebow learned, for example, that the men often spent their time on the street corner waiting for potential day employers to drive through the neighborhood and offer them work for the day (something not obvious to someone who just drives by). Through extensive discussions, Liebow also learned a lot about the men's personal relationships. Most of these men had been married once, but the marriages had ended in divorce. He also found a common theme in why many of the marriages had failed. Based on his research findings he posited the *theory of manly flaws*. "As the men look back on their broken marriages, they tend to explain the failure in terms of their personal inability or unwillingness to adjust to the built-in demands of the marriage relationship." Through in-depth discussions, Liebow learned that the reasons men initially gave for their marriages ending often changed when the discussion was allowed to progress. After a time the reasons shifted from seemingly superficial excuses to concrete examples of not being able to deal with the expectations the role of husband carries. These men were simply ashamed of not being able to provide for their families, not being able to be the head of the household, or to be the "man of the house." Because of an inability to live up to the expected role, leaving was easier than staying.

OBSERVATION

Liebow's study involved observation and in-depth interviewing. **Observation** is the basis of all scientific research and an essential part of qualitative studies. In qualitative research, observation occurs in a natural setting. It allows the researcher to study the social phenomenon of interest in its natural environment: students in a lunch room, workers in an office building, or fans at a football game. Instead of asking people about their behavior, the researcher witnesses it firsthand. Observations in this sense are systematic, not casual. That is the observations are taken in a precise way, adhering to established guidelines.

Participant Observation

Participation observation is a method of inquiry where the researcher is an active participant in the social setting. Participant observation is much more common in qualitative work than pure observation (as a nonparticipant). As an active participant, the researcher engages in activities with the group under study. This method allows researchers to engross themselves in the group's world. How group members interact with one another, the apparent organizational structure, who surfaces as a leader of the group, and so on, can all be studied from an insider's perspective.

Sometimes the researcher will tell the others that she is conducting research; this is called **overt participation**. Other times though, this information is kept hidden, or **covert participation**. The concern with overt observation is that people will act differently if they know they are being watched (recall the Hawthorne Effect). Clearly a researcher wants to capture the reality of a situation and not one that has been modified due to outside influences. Because of this desire, in some situations researchers believe that covert participation is necessary. One famous example of covert participant observation is that undertaken by Erving Goffman in his study of mental hospitals. Goffman worked as the Assistant Athletic Director in an asylum for the mentally ill. His research, published as *Stigma* in 1968, was mainly covert; only a couple of staff members were apprised of what he has doing. Through this method he was able to uncover the "unofficial reality" of life in a mental institution.

Many researchers, however, believe that covert participation is simply unethical and should never be conducted, under any circumstances. These researchers believe that people always have a right to know if someone is studying them and that not telling them is simply unacceptable. Those solidly opposed to covert participation argue that rapport can be established between observers

Informed Consent

While many argue that a participant observer must always inform people about the research project and obtain informed consent, there are clearly some situations where this is simply not feasible. Sociologist James Wright was a participant observer during his research on NASCAR culture. To conduct the participant observation he would attend NASCAR races, hang out before the race with other fans, and sit in the stands during the race. Clearly there is no way he could have informed all of the spectators about what he was doing and gotten consent from all of them to participate in his research. While not technically covert in his research, he never told anyone what he was doing nor did he obtain consent.

The Gatekeeper

Betsy Swart had to gain access to a group she was not a member of when conducting research for her dissertation on gendered abuse in Kenyan slums. The main struggle Betsy faced was being a white woman from the Western world—an outsider. To gain the trust of those she would be studying, she first approached the group with a Kenyan woman who was a teacher, a trusted gatekeeper. Being seen with the teacher, Betsy immediately earned an air of credibility. From this opening, she began to spend time with the group and began to ask them to tell her about their needs and what they wanted to talk about, never putting her agenda ahead of the women's well-being. After an extended period of time, the women came to trust Betsy and shared more and more information with her, including their personal diaries chronicling their abuse.

and participants within a group and that the impact of the researcher's presence can be minimal and thus not intrusive on the research conducted.

In overt participation, researchers will obtain informed consent from participants prior to beginning the research process. In covert participation, researchers may debrief subjects after the research has ended. Regardless of which type of participant observation is used, maintaining confidentiality is a primary concern.

Another matter of concern in participant observation is gaining initial access to a group. Rarely is the researcher a member of the group to be studied. Thus, securing access to a group that is to be studied often requires the assistance of a **gatekeeper**. The gatekeeper not only provides access to the group but can help assure other group members that the researcher is someone who can be allowed in, thus putting other group members at ease.

Although a gatekeeper is important (if not essential) to gaining access, the focus of the study is much broader, and the researchers must immediately begin to interact with as many members of the group as possible. If the same two or three people interact with the researcher while the remaining members stay silent, the results of the study are likely to be biased. Those two or three members may be different from other members of the group in essential ways and may have dramatically different experiences, which are not indicative of the group as a whole.

Participant observation can take a long time; in fact, a researcher may be interacting with the group being studied for a year or more because it takes time to fully understand the processes and interactions of a group. Many other factors can influence how long a study will take. For example, if the researcher discloses herself to the group as a researcher, it may take time for group members to trust her. In most cases, the researcher will also often have to learn a special language. This does not refer to foreign languages, but rather the colloquial expressions or terminology that group members use to communicate with one another. A cheerleading team, a gang, or a chess club, all have their own special language; to truly understand what is occurring, the participant observer must learn this language.

During participant observation, the researcher will not ask formal interview questions or read from a questionnaire. Instead, data will be generated through observation and informal conversations with group members. The researcher may spend considerable time thinking about what questions should be asked, but many questions evolve in the field. Most questions are generated by what the participant observer sees and hears (i.e., what group members do and what group members say).

A core function of participant observation is recording everything that is being heard and seen. Thus note taking is a core part of a participant observer's routine. Because there are so many different things that need to be recorded, most experienced researchers keep several sets of notes, a practice that is highly recommended. One set of notes should be dedicated to recording information about what is actually being observed. These notes will focus on what is being seen and heard during the observation. Another set of notes should record what the researcher is doing during the observation times (i.e., how the researcher is interacting with group members, what role the researcher is taking). The third set of notes is for the researcher to record thoughts about and responses to what has been going on. It is important to understand that participant observers are also impacted by the research process, and these notes allow researchers to process their own feelings and reactions to events and conversations and how they have been impacted by the experience.

Some researchers prefer to keep notes electronically, which certainly makes data analysis easier. Others like to write the notes by hand, typing them at a later date. In most cases notes are not taken during observation (note-taking is distracting and intrusive), so it is important for the researcher to take notes as quickly as possible after the observation session concludes. Waiting is not recommended as elapsed time can easily alter or dim memories and affect data quality.

Researchers conducting a participant observation are interested in two general types of information: explicit and tacit. **Explicit information** refers to information that is easily transmitted to others, usually in written form. Examples of explicit information are user or employee manuals. **Tacit information** on the other hand is much more difficult for outsiders to understand. Tacit information is often taken for granted by those who possess it and therefore more difficult to transmit to others. For example, consider all of the tacit knowledge of fans that regularly attend home team basketball games. If a player makes a foul shot, fans cheer. If a player makes a three pointer, there is another cheer.

Seemingly all player actions result in a choreographed crowd action. First time attendees are lost. There are, of course, no classes for fans; the cheer response to certain actions on the basketball court are simply learned over time while attending games. For a qualitative researcher, gaining as much tacit knowledge as possible is vital to a successful study.

QUALITATIVE INTERVIEWS

The interview is an extremely important, and most common, mode of qualitative data collection. Qualitative interviews differ from quantitative in-person survey interviews in that they are much less structured. The interview is allowed to flow like a conversation. Although the interviewer sometimes has a list of questions to ask, the process is not rigid. Information that is not explicitly asked about in the list of questions can surface. This can lead to new questions. Qualitative interviews allow participants to discuss what they believe is important about a topic. Since they are not being asked a specific number of questions with set answer options, information that the interviewer may not have thought even to ask can be unearthed.

Qualitative interviews can take different forms. Some studies use very unstructured qualitative interviews. Participants are asked different questions, and participants guide the discussion in many directions. While the interviewer may have certain topics to cover, the discussion is allowed to flow in a loose conversational format. Other studies employ more structured formats. In these situations, there is a set of questions that each participant will be asked. However, follow-up questions may be different for each participant and some level of freedom is maintained. In other cases, qualitative interviews are extremely structured and appear to be almost quantitative. They are still qualitative, however, because are no set answer options from which to choose and the qualitative researcher does not statistically analyze data but looks for themes and patterns in the data.

Qualitative interviews are often used with other methods, but they can also be used as a standalone method. For example, an undergraduate student and I are currently conducting qualitative interviews to study what it is like to be a homeless father with children in tow. Interviews are semi-structured in nature. That is, there is a set list of questions, but the interviews progress naturally. As long as the interviewee is discussing relevant information, the interviews progress without redirection. This approach can be challenging. Because qualitative interviews often feel like normal conversations, getting off track or going on a tangent can frequently occur; it takes a skilled interviewer to guide the conversation back on topic without making the interviewee feel dismissed.

While other methods could have been used for the study of fathers who are homeless, we chose semi-structured qualitative interviews for several reasons. First, there is very little information on this particular social phenomenon to date. Therefore the study is descriptive in nature. Second, we have not located many men who are homeless with children. This makes acquiring a large sample from which findings could be generalized impossible. Moreover, writing questions for a quantitative study would be difficult because so little about this phenomenon is currently known. Finally, we wanted to know not just what types of men are homeless in terms of basic demographics, we want to know what it is like to be a homeless father. The men in our study reside at an emergency shelter that is primarily populated by women. We wanted to know what life in this environment is like.

Interviews are often audiorecorded (as in the case above), which allows the interviewer to focus on listening to the respondent during the interview rather than focusing on taking extensive notes. These audio-recordings are typically transcribed to allow for analysis. A **transcription** is a written copy of an audio-recording. Transcriptions can be coded by hand or uploaded into a computer program which will allow for analysis (this is discussed in Chapter 8).

As noted above, there is no set structure for qualitative interviews. Some are more structured than others, but they all allow researchers to collect an immense amount of data that can be analyzed to produce a thorough understanding of a social phenomenon of interest.

ETHNOGRAPHY

Participant observation and interviews are often used in conjunction with other methods in a research study. In **ethnography**, participation observation and interviews are often used together to promote a full understanding about a group of people. Ethnography can be understood as both a research method and as a result of research. It is defined as the systematic study of human cultures. A classic ethnography in sociology is Mitchell Duneier's *Sidewalk*. This ethnography focused on a somewhat unlikely group: men who sold magazines on a sidewalk in New York City. Using observation and interviews, Duneier delved into the lives of these men that so many New Yorkers would walk past every day but never really *see*. Duneier's research explored the structure of the business, how the men went about selling the magazines, and why they chose this work. Through his research he learned about the men themselves, including the fact that some were homeless and that some had serious substance abuse issues. What casual passersby would not see was that the apparently haphazard nature of the magazine sales was actually quite structured. The men described in Duneier's study were part of a community, providing support to others in the group.

This work, and others like it, is significant because it allows readers to learn about others whom they would most likely never have the chance to understand. While people make assumptions about others all the time based on superficial observations, ethnographic works have the ability to show that what is apparent on the surface does not fully reflect the reality beneath.

FOCUS GROUPS

Focus groups have their roots in the field of marketing and are still used frequently in the marketing world. When companies are developing a product, packaging, a logo, or related items, focus groups might be convened. These focus groups provide the company with feedback about what consumers think about the ideas they are developing. While still often associated with marketing, focus groups are now used in other disciplines as well.

Focus groups have become an important method for sociologists. In a focus group, several people (usually 6–8) participate in a group discussion that is focused (hence the name) on one general topic. It is important that focus group participants have at least one thing in common, but it also best that they are not too familiar with one another. The group is led by a **moderator**, who is often the researcher. The moderator's role is to keep the conversation on topic, to ensure that all group members are participating, and to ensure that one or two members of the group are not dominating the conversation. The moderator must actively listen during the session, ask appropriate follow-up questions, or offer possible opinions that differ from those offered by group members. The group dynamic is what makes focus groups unique, and the moderator must make sure that the group stays on task.

The moderator typically works with a list of **guiding questions**. These are questions that should guide or direct the focus group. However, focus groups are not group interviews but more conversational in nature. The moderator may follow the list of guiding questions sequentially, maybe not. Oftentimes participants will bring up the topics covered in the guiding questions before the moderator does. It is important that the same questions are addressed in all focus group sessions if analysis across groups is planned, but the order does not need to be rigidly followed. Besides guiding the discussion, the moderator must ensure that everyone is participating and prevent any one person from dominating the conversation. An experienced moderator will be able to quell the domination by one participant while simultaneously eliciting the participation from the more reluctant participants.

Being in a group setting allows participants to potentially think about issues in a different way. One participant may present a way of thinking about a particular issue that the others may never have considered. The discussion that ensues will give clues as to why people hold the views that they do. This is called the **group dynamic**. This dynamic has benefits but can also have disadvantages. If one participant is particularly persuasive and the others are somewhat timid, the persuader may easily be able to convince the others that her opinion is correct. A well-trained moderator can help ensure that all opinions are validated and that all participants feel comfortable voicing their opinions even in the presence of very persuasive people.

What is also important in focus groups is what is *not* said. Unlike with telephone surveys or Internet surveys, the moderator can see all of the participants. Facial expressions, body language, and other nonverbal cues are all important data. Typically focus groups are audio- or video-recorded. As with interviews, the audio-recording is transcribed to allow for the data to be coded for themes. They are often video-recorded also to allow for a thorough analysis of the nonverbal expressions of the participants to be conducted.

Focus groups are an excellent way to allow people to discuss issues about which they may hold strong opinions, although may not be appropriate when discussing highly charged or personally sensitive topics, such as sexual abuse or health issues. In these instances, participants may be more comfortable in a more private setting, such as a one on one interview.

Often the most challenging part of conducting focus groups is recruiting participants. In this day and age of identity theft and thinly disguised sales pitches masquerading as seminars, it is not surprising that many potential participants are wary of invitations to participate in focus groups. The idea of being paid for supplying one's opinion seems too good to be true for many people. Because of the public's heightened awareness of sales tactics and fraudulent come-ons, recruitment can be a resource-intensive endeavor. Nevertheless, it is clearly essential to conducting a focus group study and must be addressed. Some approaches work better than others; all approaches need to keep in mind that no target group is identical. If conducting a focus group at a particular place of business, such as a city courthouse, recruitment can be accomplished rather easily. Recruiting college students at a certain college or residents of a particular town may require more time and additional resources.

CASE STUDY

A **case study** is a research method that involves the study of a single group, event, or person. It may seem counterintuitive that sociology, and its focus on groups and common patterns, would employ this research method, but it is quite common. *Heat Wave*, a text cited earlier, is an excellent example of a case study. The case study was prompted by the heat wave in Chicago, which resulted in the death of hundreds of people. The author relied on many methods to explore this event, including archival data analysis, statistical analysis, and interviews. This illustrates that while the focus of a case study may be a single event, the associated research often relies on many sociological research methods. One advantage to case studies is that a thorough understanding of the object under study can be achieved. The main disadvantage for case studies is that the findings may not generalize beyond the particular case being studied.

There are many different types of case studies. **Illustrative case studies** are used when trying to describe an event or specific situation. This type of case study allows readers to gain an "on the outside looking in" point of view and makes them familiar with a subject that they might have not had any contact with or prior knowledge of. The researcher basically paints a picture (illustrates) for those who are unaware of the social phenomenon being studied. An illustrative case study may examine what life is like for sweatshop workers in New York City. The purpose then would be to describe to those with no experience with this life what it is like to be a sweatshop worker.

Exploratory case studies are initiated to help *explore* any type of phenomenon before a large-scale examination begins. The purpose is to become familiar with a topic to gauge the types of questions that should be used in the research, and to then select an appropriate type of measurement before the investigation takes place. Pilot studies are often exploratory case studies. For example, a researcher might have noticed that the majority of students majoring in biology are female but that the majority of the faculty is male. An exploratory case study might examine if students are aware of this and if it has any impact on their educational experience.

The last type of case studies discussed in this chapter is **critical instance case studies**, which are used to examine a specific phenomenon of rare interest or to challenge an extremely generalized widespread claim. Following the 1999 Columbine High School massacre, researchers set forth to explain the "Columbine Effect," a phenomenon that served to "explain" each school shooting both prior to and after the Columbine shooting. Columbine is widely viewed as the "critical instance" against which all other school-shooting episodes are measured or compared. The Columbine High School massacre thus became the defining event, or critical instance, of school shootings in modern history.

As mentioned earlier, there are advantages and disadvantages to case studies. The advantages include flexibility and the opportunity to acquire deep understanding of a topic. Because of the way the method is designed, a researcher can stress exploration of the topic that is being examined (rather than making predictions) and focus on issues as they surface during research.

Some disadvantages include generalizability, intersubjectivity, and replication. In terms of generalizability, because the researcher is studying a limited case or group very thoroughly, it is difficult to apply the findings to society in a general sense. One such example is in Elijah Anderson's book *Code of the Street*, which recounts a qualitative case study examining a particular neighborhood in Philadelphia. As Anderson's research spanned several months in this one area, any findings could be applied only to that particular neighborhood and not other inner-city neighborhoods. **Intersubjectivity** refers to a researcher's own interpretation of data including interviews, interaction, and observations. Two people viewing the same thing (even if it is as simple as observing people in the park) will take away different impressions of the experience based on their respective world views. **Replication**, which is when a researcher conducts a study that will be the same as a study someone else has previously conducted, is especially difficult in case studies. This is because case studies are typically based on observations as they happen, making them nearly impossible to replicate in a different study. If the study cannot be replicated, there is no way to determine if the results are accurate.

ETHNOMETHODOLOGICAL METHODS

Ethnomethodology is a subfield in sociology that focuses on how people go about constructing order in their everyday lives. Thus the purpose of research for ethnomethodologists is to examine how people produce and organize their everyday interactions with a particular focus on the methods that people use to do this. There are two qualitative methods that have come from ethnomethodology: breaching experiments and conversation analysis.

Breaching Experiments

Breaching experiments are most often associated with the work of Harold Garfinkel. The basic idea in a **breaching experiment** is to purposefully violate an established cultural expectation of behavior, or norm (what we take for granted and do usually without giving it much thought). For example, most students would not walk onto a classroom on the first day and lie down on the floor. Sitting in a desk is an established norm for student behavior. An important note: Breaching experiments are not about doing anything illegal but rather illuminating the rules that we live by that we do not typically even realize are in place.

In one such experiment Garfinkel instructed his students to return to their parents' homes and act as though they were strangers. Complying with these instructions, the students asked what time breakfast would be served, where they should sleep, and other questions to which they should clearly have known the answers. Students were told to do this for up to an hour. The students who participated reported that their parents were quite confused by what was occurring. Normal interaction between parent and child broke down, illuminating the unwritten rules that ordinarily guide these interactions.

Another famous experiment was conducted by students of social psychologist Stanley Milgram. They were instructed to go on to a subway in New York City and ask people to give up their seats for them, even if there were other seats available. The students reported feeling very uneasy about participating in this exercise as breaking such social norms can make all involved uncomfortable. Interestingly the majority of those asked to give up their seats did so, even though the students provided no reason why the riders should give up their seats.

Methods of Breaching Experiments

Common activities in breaching experiments include:

- Facing backwards in an elevator (everyone knows we are supposed to face the door!)
- "Shopping" out of someone else's shopping cart in the grocery store
- Sitting in the front of the classroom on the floor instead of sitting at a desk
- Ordering a "whopper" at a McDonald's
- Trying to "tip" friends or family members when they do something nice for you, such as getting you a drink or a snack
- Offering to pay more for an item at a store

Although breaching experiments can be quite humorous, they illustrate an important point in sociology. Many of our norms and standards for behavior are so ingrained that we don't think about them. They are simply things that "everybody knows." But such norms and behavioral standards are not innate; they are learned. The breaching experiments bring these rules to light. These standards for interaction, the rules we take for granted, are the focus of ethnomethodologists.

Conversation Analysis

Breaching experiments are not the only research method to come out of ethnomethodology. Another method is called **conversation analysis**, which uses audio or video recordings or written transcripts of naturally occurring conversations as sources of data. Unlike with some other qualitative methods, the researcher does not participate in the conversations that are recorded. In this sense the conversation analysis is a specific type of an unobtrusive measure.

One example of a study relying on conversation analysis is a study conducted by Don Zimmerman and Candace West who analyzed conversations in a college community. They found that in same-sex conversations, interruptions were distributed fairly evenly among the speakers. In the cross-sex conversations, however, contrary to the belief that women talk and interrupt others more than men do while speaking, men were responsible for 96 percent of the interruptions. Zimmerman and West concluded that men deny equal status to women as conversational partners. By interrupting, men prevent women from talking and gain the floor for their own discussion. Women who try to interrupt men are seen as rude, domineering, and bossy. It is interesting to note that most people will not admit to or even realize that they engage in this behavior, but through conversation analysis, such patterns such as the gender differences within conversations, can be brought to light.

QUALITATIVE CONTENT ANALYSIS

Like its quantitative counterpart, qualitative content analysis is a research method in which social artifacts are analyzed. It differs from quantitative content analysis in several key ways. First, the objective in a qualitative content analysis is not to quantify but to explore meaning. Second, in a quantitative content analysis the researcher begins with a list of specifics for which he or she will be searching (e.g., the race or gender of models in print advertisements). In qualitative content analysis, the researcher does not typically start with a list of criteria. Instead, the researcher records the themes that become apparent as the materials are analyzed. The process is inductive as opposed to deductive. A third difference concerns the results of the research. Whereas quantitative content analyses often include statistical findings, qualitative content analyses often result in a collection of themes or the development of a theory.

Markella B. Rutherford conducted a qualitative content analysis by examining childrearing advice present in 300 articles in *Parents* magazine. Focusing on children's autonomy, Rutherford took a random sample of articles and began coding the articles looking for discussions on this issue. Whenever she found the subject mentioned, she would use a code or codes to summarize the passage. Rutherford explains how she coded the articles: "For example, an advice column included a reader's question about her toddler's difficult eating habits; the expert's answer discussed both children's choices about what to eat and children's testing of limits set by parents . . . . This advice scenario was coded as pertaining both to activities of daily living and to challenging parental authority."

At the end of the analysis, Rutherford concluded that there has been an increase over time in the promotion of children's autonomy in many ways, including activities of daily living, personal appearance, and defiance of parents. She also concluded that children's "freedom of movement" has been restricted over time due to parents' concern for children's safety.

SUMMARY

Qualitative methods are an important part of social inquiry. They allow for a deep understanding of social reality. Because they do not produce statistically generalizable findings, some discount their importance. However, their worth is clear. What is important is that they are applied rigorously, with attention to consistency, sampling methods, and bias. Reducing bias is of utmost concern in all research but is particularly important in qualitative work because the researcher is so actively and deeply involved in the data collection process.

Qualitative work within sociology has illuminated nearly all of the social problems that we are concerned with: poverty, homelessness, drug abuse, criminal involvement, and so forth. Qualitative methods in these areas have moved past demographic information and causal relationships into an understanding of how and why people are impacted in a particular way, and most importantly what it is like to be someone in particular situations.

Further Reading

Berg, Bruce L.. *Qualitative Research Methods for the Social Sciences*. 6th ed. Boston: Pearson/Allyn & Bacon, 2007.

DeWalt, Kathleen Musante, and Billie R. DeWalt. *Participant Observation: A Guide for Fieldworkers*. 2nd ed. Lanham, Md.: Rowman & Littlefield, 2011.

Duneier, Mitchell, and Ovie Carter. *Sidewalk*. New York: Farrar, Straus and Giroux, 1999.

Emerson, Robert M., Rachel I. Fretz, and Linda L. Shaw. *Writing Ethnographic Fieldnotes*. Chicago: University Of Chicago Press, 1995.

Garfinkel, Harold. *Studies in Ethnomethodology*. Reprint. ed. Cambridge: Polity Press, 1999.

Liebow, Elliot. *Tally's Corner: A Study of Negro Streetcorner Men*. New ed. Lanham, Md.: Rowman & Littlefield, 2003.

Lofland, John. *Analyzing Social Settings: A Guide to Qualitative Observation and Analysis*. 4th ed. Belmont, Calif.: Wadsworth/Thomson Learning, 2006.

Morgan, David L. *Focus Groups as Qualitative Research*. 2nd ed. Thousand Oaks, Calif.: Sage Publications, 2008.

Rubin, Herbert J., and Irene Rubin. *Qualitative Interviewing: The Art of Hearing Data*. 2nd ed. Thousand Oaks, Calif.: Sage Publications, 2005.

CHAPTER 4

APPLIED SOCIOLOGY AND EVALUATION RESEARCH

There are two overarching schools of thought in sociology. There is "pure sociology," which produces work for academic or scholarly audiences. Then there is "applied sociology," which produces work from which people outside of academia can benefit. In this chapter we explore applied sociology in general and focus on one of the most common forms of applied sociology—evaluation research.

APPLIED SOCIOLOGY

Applied sociology uses sociological methods and theories and applies them outside of academia. Applied sociology can encompass many different things but in a basic sense it consists of sociologists that use what they know to assist agencies, people, or groups. An applied sociologist who studies domestic violence may work with a domestic violence shelter, may serve as an expert witness in trials that involve domestic violence, or may write a letter to the editor of a local paper on a story about domestic violence. A sociologist who studies drug abuse may work with a local agency by providing instruction on the best practices in drug abuse treatment. This is done to ensure that the program staff is serving people to the best of their ability. All of these examples take the researcher out of the university setting and into the real world where sociological theory is put into practice.

A real-world example of applied sociology in action might be a large food bank trying to determine where to open new food outlets. The food bank wants to open the outlets in areas with the greatest need, the so called "food deserts," or areas where residents have little or no access to healthy foods. The food bank has identified five neighborhoods with high needs. These five were selected after an examination of characteristics such as poverty level and average household income. The researcher assigned to the problem begins by identifying all of the food outlets that are in the area (grocery stores, convenience stores, and the like). Once these outlets are identified, the next task is to determine what the outlets sell. To do this, the researcher creates a checklist that contains 70 products (orange juice, fresh tomatoes, etc). She then assembles a team of researchers, each armed with the checklist, who are instructed to check yes or no for each item, depending on whether it is available or not, in each outlet. In the end, the data are compiled to identify the areas in the greatest need. The food bank then uses this information to decide where to open new food outlets.

One of the important differences between applied research and academic research is that applied research is geared toward solving a concrete problem. In the food bank example, the researcher was not testing hypotheses. There was no review of the literature. There was no theoretical grounding. There was a client that needed to make a decision and wanted to make an informed decision that would result in the greatest benefit to the community.

Applied research can also be a part of public policy decisions. For example, researchers conducted focus groups as a part of an applied project to assess homeless persons' opinions about the proposed relocation of the homeless shelter where they were currently staying. The existing shelter was located downtown in a major metropolitan area and had convenient access to services and transportation. Three possible new locations had been proposed and the researchers wanted to know what it would mean to the day-to-day existence of the shelter residents (about half of whom were women and children) if the homeless center were moved out of downtown? They wanted to determine, in particular, how the children's lives would be impacted.

These applied researchers conducted focus groups to ensure that the voices of the clients that would be impacted were included in the political debate. The focus groups dealt with issues of time, inconvenience, cost, safety, relative isolation, and the psychological stressors associated with each of the proposed new locations. They learned from shelter residents that relocation from the downtown area to a more remote site was a cause for concern. The residents feared it would cause them to miss buses, miss appointments, be late picking their children up from childcare, or miss work. None of the three proposed locations was viewed as preferable to the current location (although all participants said they would go wherever the new shelter happened to be). In the end the shelter was not moved.

As you can see, applied research allows sociologists to use their skills and knowledge to serve agencies and disadvantaged populations. Applied research

Evaluations are not always about policies

While most evaluations measure the effectiveness of programs or policies or gauge the efficacy of agency processes, this is not always the case. Some evaluations can be likened to customer satisfaction surveys. Consider the evaluation of a conference. The conference hosts want to know how people feel about the conference: Did they enjoy the sessions, the speakers, the accommodations? Hosts also want to know which sessions were most popular, and whether people will attend next year's conference. An evaluation can answer these questions. In the evaluation, for example, conference attendees can fill out forms after each session, offering their opinion about each session, and these can be compiled and compared with one another to determine which sessions were the most popular and which were the least well received.

can also be used as useful information for policy makers. Applied researchers spend time "in the field" and outside of the halls of academia because they believe that good research can have an impact on society at large.

EVALUATION RESEARCH

One facet of applied sociology is evaluation research. **Evaluation research** is a specific type of social research that many applied sociologists conduct. In essence, evaluation research examines the effects or advisability of a social policy or program. It is similar to other types of research (or "basic" research) in that it requires the same methodological standards and principles. However evaluation research differs from basic research in some key ways.

One key way in which evaluation research differs from basic research is that evaluation research typically involves **stakeholders**. Stakeholders are individuals, groups, or organizations that have a vested interest in the program or policy that is being evaluated. Three groups of stakeholders are often key in an evaluation: program clients, program personnel and administrators, and the funders. Program clients are the people who directly benefit from a program whereas program personnel and administrators derive their livelihoods from the program or intervention being evaluated. The funders are the people whose money is being spent to pay for the program. As you may guess, the interests of these three stakeholder groups are seldom the same and are often in conflict, so evaluators must remain objective in the face of potentially competing opinions and interests.

Program clients often receive some value from a particular program even though it may not be achieving the desired effect or attaining set goals. People who work on behalf of the program are often passionate about the program and are convinced that it "works," even though it may not in an objective sense. Funders want to know that they are receiving ample return on the investment, that program goals are being achieved, and that their money is being spent in the most effective possible way. The evaluator's job is not to tell anyone what they want to hear but rather to scientifically evaluate a program or policy.

A second way evaluation research differs from basic research is that outcomes of evaluations often have very concrete results. Evaluations are used in making decisions about continuing, expanding, contracting, or even discontinuing programs. They can be used to provide information to program personnel and policy makers about changes that should be made while a program or policy change is underway. Likewise, they can be used to increase the effectiveness of program management, enhance implementation, or to sharpen the focus on populations that are targeted by the program or policy.

Unlike with basic research, evaluation is often a required component in a program or policy. Funders, such as agencies within the federal government or private foundations, may require an evaluator to be involved with a given program or project. The evaluator in this context ensures that the program is being implemented properly and that outcomes are being met. The evaluator can also ensure that the program is effectively using the funds that the program received.

A final key difference between evaluations and basic research is that evaluations are often very political. Pure sociology is primarily of academic interest; in contrast, evaluations (and particularly their outcomes) may be of interest to a great many people with no connection to the academic world. Among those interested parties are politicians and other policy makers. A program, for example, might be deemed ineffective at the conclusion of an evaluation study, but might have wide community support. In this case eliminating or even radically

Sesame Street

You are no doubt familiar with the television program, *Sesame Street*. The show was primarily designed to target disadvantaged preschool children who had not received any formal education, in the hopes of better preparing them for school. After its first two years on the air, the show was evaluated to determine if the goals had been achieved. The evaluation found that viewers of *Sesame Street* scored better on assessments of basic skills and cognitive activity, and that those who watched the show most often had significantly higher scores compared to those who watched less frequently. The evaluation also found that disadvantaged children watched less often than more privileged children. Thus the program was successful, but it was not reaching the group it was intended to reach.

Head Start

Head Start, the largest federally funded early childhood program in the country, provides preschool education to disadvantaged children. It has been active for over 45 years and is very popular. It has also had mixed results in terms of its effectiveness in the many evaluations that have been done to date. Some evaluations, including the most recent, have found that children who have participated in Head Start have similar levels of academic achievement as other disadvantaged children who were never in the program. Nevertheless, the program continues (at least for now) to be funded and is widely supported.

changing the program may not be politically advantageous (the reverse is true as well). Clearly the research is not the only consideration, especially when you consider that many of the issues that applied sociologists deal with are highly politicized (e.g., social welfare programs). Evaluators will often become involved in the related political discussions.

There are several types of evaluations that can be conducted. They are generally categorized as either formative or summative. **Formative evaluations** assess the worth of a program or policy before or during its implementation. These types of evaluations may help shape the way a program is delivered or even help determine what types of programs or policies should be implemented in the first place. **Summative evaluations** focus on the outcomes of programs or policies. These type of evaluations occur after a program or policy has been implemented and measures the manner in which it was implemented and its overall effectiveness. Depending on the program or policy, several different components may be combined to form the overall evaluation strategy.

Formative Evaluations

There are several different types of formative evaluations. Three of the most common—needs assessments, process or implementation evaluations, and theory driven evaluations—are discussed here. Each of these evaluation types can be done individually or aspects from each can be combined into an overall formative evaluation design. Formative evaluations can be invaluable for programs as a means of informing those involved how they can be more efficiently implemented and delivered.

Needs Assessments

Needs assessments can be used to determine, on a community level, what the most pressing needs for that community are. They can also be used to study a specific issue or need in a community, to help understand how great the need may be, who is in need, and the like. That is, a needs assessment could be undertaken to determine which issue (or issues) merits priority attention, whether it be crime, poverty, education, or the like. At the issue level, evaluations can be used to determine how much need there is for a particular intervention, who may benefit from the intervention program, and what types of programs may be most beneficial. If a group of people in a community want to address the academic performance of children in school, they might conduct a needs assessment to determine how many children need assistance, at what grade levels students struggle the most, and what types of interventions are expected to have the greatest impact.

A needs evaluation also could be used to help determine what new program a multifaceted agency may want to implement. Let's say there is an agency that serves the needs of the elderly. The agency already has a program that delivers meals to elderly clients as well as a program that provides social opportunities for seniors. What should the new program focus on? What is most needed? Needs assessments can ensure that additional programs will fill in gaps in existing services or even determine whether there is a demand (or need) for a new program.

Needs assessments can also help shape priorities for communities. Large funding institutions in communities receive many requests from agencies for financial assistance. How do they decide which agencies to fund? One consideration might be which agencies are addressing the greatest needs in the community. Because all communities are unique, a needs assessment can determine what issues are paramount. A needs assessment of this type might involve several different data sources. Statistical data examining the characteristics of the community would be important. Are there certain social problems that are particularly prevalent? What do residents think is most important? Community stakeholders? All of these sources of data can be analyzed to determine which needs should take priority.

Implementation Evaluation

When a program is up and running and providing services to clients, it is rarely identical to the program that the founders designed on paper. Sometimes there is only a slight resemblance. Significant differences between the initial design and the actual implementation of a program might provide one explanation for the failure of some programs to achieve significant results. In connection with this, applied sociology often uses a process or **implementation evaluation,** which focuses on the way a program was implemented.

There are many reasons why a program is not implemented in the way it was designed. The program could have been designed in a way that was not viable or feasible given the structure of the agency as a whole; there may be bureaucratic barriers in place that prevent program implementation, or unanticipated conditions or outside influences that hinder the program's proper implementation. When a program or policy analysis depends on quasi-experimental methods, it can fail at the point of randomization of clients or participants. For example, research that tests the effectiveness of programs serving people sometimes require that clients be randomized into control and treatment groups. The treatment group receives services or a certain kind of service, such as free meal vouchers in a school lunch program, while the control group receives no services or limited services. Program personnel may be responsible for randomly assigning clients to one of the two groups. However, program personnel may let their own sentiments about "worthy" and "unworthy" clients override the randomizing process. If this occurs (and it has been known to), then the implementation of the program is compromised and the experiment is no longer valid. In our example, staff members assisting in such an experiment may hand out vouchers to students who are polite and friendly or whom they know personally, whereas students who are viewed as troublemakers will not get vouchers. This leads to a skewed sample of recipients as the process is no longer random.

Programs that require staff to integrate new techniques can fail because the staff persists in using the same old techniques, even if told about the importance of using the new. Moreover, if new standards are developed but staff members continue to use the old, the effectiveness of the program cannot be evaluated on its merits because it was not properly implemented. More generally, the real world finds ways to impinge in unexpected and often unwanted ways on any policy initiative and program development. The failure to anticipate such impingements has caused many programs and policies to fail.

One of the best examples of the importance of implementation evaluations is a study that Loftin and McDowall conducted on the effects of the Detroit mandatory sentencing law. The policy-as-designed required a mandatory two year "add on" to the prison sentence of any person convicted of a felony involving a firearm. This means that if someone sentenced to 10 years for a crime and the crime in question involved a gun, the actual sentence would be 12 years. Contrary to expectation, the rate of firearms crime did not decline after the law was enacted, but the average sentence length also did not increase. Implementation analysis provided the reason. Judges, well aware of the overcrowded conditions in the state's prisons, were not willing to increase average prison sentences. On the other hand, state law required that two years be added to sentences for criminal acts involving firearms. To resolve the dilemma, judges in firearms cases would begin by reducing the primary sentence (that is, the sentence for the crime itself) by two or so years and then adding the mandated two-year add-on. The judges remained in technical compliance with policy, the letter of the law was followed, but the overall sentence remained about the same.

Theory-Driven Evaluations

Theory-driven evaluations seek to ascertain what the underlying theory of a particular program is, and if that underlying theory is logical given what we know about the issue. All programs have an underlying theory, even if it has never been acknowledged. It is important to understanding that all policies and programs are based on a causal theory—either explicit or implicit—that links specific program components to the intended goals or outcomes of a given program. To understand an underlying program theory, evaluators need to ask what assumptions, steps, causal sequences, behavioral changes, and logical links guide a program. Researchers can then see whether the connections between program design and goals are consistent. The "analysis of program theory" is therefore an analysis of the logical, conceptual, and empirical adequacy of the causal assumptions that guide a program.

Consider the theory of a program that wants to help build the self-esteem of young girls by providing peer mentorship. The theory, in this case, is that peer mentorship can lead to an increase in self-esteem. Is this an accurate underlying theory? Is there something else that should be done in addition to, or in place of, peer mentorship to increase self-esteem of the girls in the program? A theory driven evaluation examines the underlying program theory and objectively assesses the validity of the theoretical assumptions.

Summative Evaluations

While formative evaluations focus on the design and implementation of programs and policies, summative evaluations focus on the outcomes of programs and policies and evaluate the various levels of effectiveness of a program or policy. These evaluations typically occur once a program is well established and its merits can be objectively assessed. There are several types of summative evaluations; this chapter discusses three: outcome evaluations, impact evaluations, and cost benefit analyses.

Outcome Evaluations

Outcome evaluations focus on the stated outcomes that a program or policy was designed to meet. The outcome evaluation determines if there was a positive change as a result of the implemented program or policy and answers questions such as: Did the program accomplish what is stated it would? Was the policy effective? Did the intervention successfully intervene? Programs or policies are often developed with clearly defined measurable outcomes. This type of evaluation is very useful in objectively determining the success of a program and usually involves quantitative data although qualitative methods are sometimes used to supplement the numerical results.

For instance, an outcome evaluation was used to evaluate the effectiveness of a program for 30 students in an alternative high school. The program provided tutoring and mentoring services and had clearly defined outcomes,

And the answer was?

The outcome evaluation discussed here found that the alternative high school program that included tutoring and mentoring met all its outcomes. In addition, this program resulted in a statistically significant increase in GPA among participants.

which included the following: the number of students that should graduate within four years, the average GPA that should be achieved by the students, and the number of students who were expected to go on to college after graduation. To determine if outcomes were being met, student files were reviewed quarterly and data were complied. The results were compared against the outcome expectations.

Impact Evaluations

Impact evaluations are similar to outcome evaluations. They differ in that impact evaluations measure not just the intended and stated outcomes, but the larger potential impact the program or policy had. Sometimes these effects were intended, other times they were not. However, if a program has positive effects (even if these are unanticipated and unintended effects), it may be deemed an important program or policy that should continue.

An example of an impact evaluation was the evaluation of a residential substance abuse treatment program for homeless people in New Orleans. Homeless alcoholics and drug addicts were enrolled in a treatment program that ranged from 7 days to 13 months to determine the effects of time in treatment on various outcomes. The outcomes that were assessed included sobriety, employment, housing stability, and family reintegration. Researchers found modest positive effects of "days in treatment" on sobriety but generally no effect on the other outcomes.

Cost Benefit Analysis

A **cost-benefit analysis** is not unique to the world of evaluation research. This type of analysis is often undertaken to assess "bang for the buck." You have no doubt undertaken cost-benefit analyses in your own life. Is that new outfit worth the cost? You might figure how many times you will wear it in a season and how long you expect it to last. This analysis can help you decide if the outfit is a worthwhile purchase. In sociological evaluations, cost-benefit analyses measure the worth of programs and their overall costs. Programs may be very successful at meeting their intended outcomes, but if they are prohibitively expensive, they will most likely not remain active, particularly if they require funding from outside sources.

Take for example a teen pregnancy prevention program. A cost-benefit analysis would assess how much it costs to provide services to each young woman and compare that amount to how much it costs the community to support pregnant teenagers. The analysis might include how often pregnant teens use local social services and local emergency rooms for medical care. It would also need to measure long-term effects. The cost of providing care for clients in the program that did not become pregnant as teens would be compared to the costs incurred by teens in similar circumstances who did become pregnant. Finally, the program costs might be compared to the cost of running comparable programs to determine if they are reasonable.

Clearly, a cost-benefit analysis of this sort is much more complicated than one for a personal purchase decision, but the concept remains the same. No matter how successful a program is, the costs must be justifiable. And on the flip side, an unsuccessful program is usually not valuable, no matter how low the costs.

Comprehensive Evaluation

Oftentimes more than one type of evaluation will be conducted as a part of a single study. A comprehensive program or policy evaluation will address five specific categories: 1) needs assessment, 2) assessment of program theory, 3) process and implementation, 4) impact assessment and program outcomes, and 5) cost efficiency. A comprehensive evaluation will therefore address the following questions:

1. What problem is this program or policy targeting?
2. What indicators are there that this program or policy can successfully target this problem?
3. How has the policy or program been implemented? Is the implemented program like the one that was designed?
4. Is the program reaching the people it was designed to reach?
5. What are the effects of the program? What difference, if any, did the program make?
6. All things considered, was this a worthwhile investment of resources?

One such evaluation was conducted on a nonprofit organization that provides educational and social support to economically disadvantaged minority men. The program had been in existence for two years when the comprehensive evaluation was undertaken. The evaluator addressed all of the questions listed above to assist the program in delivering services in a cost-efficient and effective way, to focus services on specific target populations, and to determine the effects of the program thus far. Many methods were involved in the evaluation, including a review of the legal documents written when the agency was initially formed, interviews with stakeholders, focus groups with clients, analysis of client files, and analysis of program costs. Once the process was completed, the evaluator provided conclusions and recommendations to the program staff. One of the evaluator's most important findings was that the program was investing a large share of resources on clients that would never return after an initial visit. To counter this, the program now requires that all prospective clients attend an orientation session (scheduled one day after the initial visit) to ensure that clients are serious enough to make the effort to come back. Once the client has attended the mandatory orientation, he or she becomes eligible to receive services.

UTILIZATION OF APPLIED SOCIOLOGY AND EVALUATION RESULTS
In the above example, the results of the evaluation were used by program staff to make improvements. This is often the case with program evaluations. In terms of evaluations regarding policies, however, literature on the subject of evaluation research confirms that there is chronic frustration that policy analysis rarely seems to have any significant impact on policy. Many reasons for this have been identified. One of the most important is timeliness. Good research takes time whereas policy decisions are often made quickly, well before the results of the analysis are available.

A second factor inhibiting the utilization of policy studies is that research is seldom unequivocal. Even the best-designed and best-executed policy research will be accompanied by numerous caveats, conditions, and qualifications that limit policy inferences one may draw from them. Policy makers, of course, prefer simple declarative conclusions, but policy research rarely accommodates this preference.

Finally, even under the most favorable conditions, the scientific results of policy analyses are but one among many inputs into the policy-making process. There are, in addition, normative, economic, political, ethical, pragmatic, and ideological inputs that must be accommodated, and in the process of accommodation, the influence of scientific research is often obscured to the point where it can no longer be recognized. It should not be inferred from this that the sociological analysis has not been utilized, only that the research results are only one voice in a very noisy conversation.

SUMMARY
Applied sociology and evaluation research allow sociologists to use their skills outside of academia. For many sociologists this work is immensely rewarding because they can see their efforts effect change in the "real world." Research in these fields relies on the same methods used in all social research. The difference is the real-world impact that results from applied sociology and evaluation research can produce.

Further Reading

Langton, Phyllis Ann, and Dianne Anderson Kammerer. *Practicing Sociology in the Community: A Student's Guide.* Upper Saddle River, N.J.: Pearson Prentice Hall, 2004.

Patton, Michael Quinn. *Qualitative Research and Evaluation Methods.* 3rd ed. Thousand Oaks, Calif.: Sage Publications, 2001.

Rossi, Peter H., Mark W. Lipsey, and Howard E. Freeman. *Evaluation: A Systematic Approach.* 7th ed. Thousand Oaks, Calif.: Sage, 2003.

Steele, Stephen F., and Jammie Price. *Applied Sociology: Terms, Topics, Tools, and Tasks.* 2nd. ed. Belmont, Calif.: Thomson/Wadsworth, 2008.

CHAPTER 5

LESSER KNOWN METHODS

As society continues to change and evolve, so does the way that sociologists conduct research. Although we still continue to use many of the methods that we have been using for over a century, some of the ways these methods are applied have changed. For example, while surveying has remained an important method in quantitative research, many surveys are now conducted online. Advances in technology are revolutionizing survey methods in other ways too. New technology has done more than just changed surveying; it has created or made possible entirely new methods of sociological research. All of this has opened up an extensive range of new and exciting ways to study the social world.

This chapter will discuss some of the new research methods that are being used in sociology, including some of the lesser known methods that are often controversial but are praised by some as interesting and novel approaches to exploring the social world in different ways. The purpose here is not to provide an exhaustive list of all methods used in the field but rather to show a diverse range of methods that are being used in contemporary sociological research.

MIXED METHODS
The first methodology addressed in this section is an approach that combines two or more methods and is aptly named mixed methods. Using more than one type of research method in a research study is not new, but it is a growing trend because many sociologists have come to believe that no single method can

adequately explain a social phenomenon or answer all of the questions that lead to a better understanding of that phenomenon.

Mixed methods usually involve both quantitative and qualitative methods in a study. This approach, however, might just as easily involve using two or more quantitative methods or two or more qualitative methods in a single study.

Using more than one method in research is a form of **triangulation**. The concept of triangulation comes from the mathematical principles of a triangle. In sociological research the term is used to describe application or use of two or more methods, theories, or multiple research teams. Triangulation is considered a useful way of producing reliable results because those results can be validated through different means.

Sociologist Julia Brannen discussed how triangulation works in social research. Brannen underscored that the idea is not for one method to "verify" the other but that methods should complement one another. In the passage below, she explains how results of different methods can be used together in a study:

(1) Elaboration or expansion—for example qualitative data analysis may exemplify how patterns based on quantitative data analysis apply in particular cases. Here the use of one type of data analysis adds to the understanding being gained by another.

(2) Initiation—the use of a first method sparks new hypotheses or research questions that can be pursued using a different method.

(3) Complementarity—qualitative and quantitative results are treated as different beasts. Each type of data analysis enhances the other. Together the data analyses from the two methods are juxtaposed and generate complementary insights that together create a bigger picture.

(4) Contradictions—where qualitative data and quantitative findings conflict. Exploring contradictions between different types of data assumed to reflect the same phenomenon may lead to an interrogation of the methods and to discounting of one method in favour of another (in terms of assessments of validity or reliability).

TECHNOLOGY-DRIVEN METHODS

Whereas the mixed-methods approach to sociological research is not new, other methods are. The majority of these methods, including the ones that will be discussed in this section, are products of new and evolving technologies.

GIS Mapping

One technology-driven method is **Global Information Systems (GIS)**. A GIS system is a computer system that can manage, analyze, and display data based on location. There are several different GIS programs available to researchers.

GIS technology is used by cartographers, geologists, geographers, urban planners, and others who work in fields that involve understanding spatial arrangements and relationships. In this connection, GIS technology has been gaining in popularity as a method for sociologists to better understand the spatial relationship between variables of interest.

For example, GIS technology is being used in the study of crime because this technique can answer questions about where crimes are concentrated. It also lends itself to expanded research that relates to additional variables of interest. One example of this is sociologist Christa Polczynski Olson's GIS analysis of the relationship between homelessness and crime. The two are often assumed to be related but little objective research has been done to assess and confirm the relationship because it is often difficult to obtain accurate data to address the topic. GIS mapping has proved to be a useful method for delving into this particular topic. In Olson's research study, the overarching question was: "Are there more crimes occurring around homeless shelters as compared to other areas in the city?" To begin this analysis, Polczynski Olson obtained arrest data. Using this arrest data, she mapped all arrests and then added homeless shelter locations to the map. Working with this composite she performed an analysis to determine if there is indeed more crime around homeless shelters than in other areas of the city. Polczynski Olson found that certain crimes, like drug violations and ordinance crimes (such as sleeping on park benches) were more prevalent around homeless shelters. Violent and sexual crimes, however, were not.

GIS is not only a useful tool in studying crime but can be used to study various topics and can be invaluable in applied sociology projects. Consider the following example. A social service agency wants to know where to build a new facility so that it is accessible to people who use the city bus system. To find a suitable site, the agency can use a GIS map of the city showing all of the bus stations (easy to do) and then another GIS map with all existing social service agency facilities, which can be overlaid on top of the bus map. This layered map will clearly show all of the areas where there are no existing facilities and will also show which currently existing facilities are not easily accessible by bus. This information can be used to determine where a new facility (one that will be accessible to potential clients) should be located.

It is very likely that GIS will continue to grow in popularity as a method for sociologists to use in their research. Because spatial relationships are often integral to the research, particularly in certain areas of study like criminology and urban sociology, this technology is extremely useful.

Audio Computer Assisted Self-Interviewing

Another new method used in social research is **Audio Computer Assisted Self-Interviewing** (ACASI), which is a type of self-administered survey question-

Telephone Surveys

There are several variations of Audio Computer Assisted Self-Interviewing (ACASI). One of these is Telephone-Audio Computer Assisted Self-Interviewing (T-ACASI). In this mode there are no laptops involved. Instead respondents answer voice-digitized questions by pressing keys on a touchtone telephone or by speaking the answers, which are recognized by the computer system. Thus there is also no telephone interviewer involved. Some studies have shown that respondents are more apt to disclose socially undesirable behavior in a T-ACASI survey than they would during a traditional phone survey.

naire often combined with a Computer Assisted Telephone Interviewing (CATI) system. Respondents are given a laptop (often touch screen) that has the survey questionnaire in a preloaded survey program. The respondents take the survey just as they would take an Internet survey. This method eliminates the need for an interviewer (and data entry). It has also been suggested that this type of survey can be more amenable to respondents when the topics addressed are of a sensitive nature. Thus problems associated with social desirability influencing responses may be less prevalent in this type of surveying than in face-to-face or telephone surveys.

Studies focusing on several sensitive topics including drug abuse and risky sexual behavior have been conducted using ACASI. Because there is a high level of privacy for respondents with this mode, it is a particularly appropriate method for researching such topics. Many studies that evaluate the usability and reliability of ACASI as compared to other modes have been conducted. One such study examined the usefulness of ACASI in collecting information from a cohort of American Indians. The information collected included medical backgrounds, dietary habits, and extent of physical activity. Although nearly one-third of the participants had not used a computer in the past year, the overwhelmingly majority found them to be enjoyable (96 percent), easy to use (97 percent), and the preferred mode for future surveys (83 percent). Based on these responses, this study (and others like it) found that ACASI is a very promising technology that sociologists can use to collect data for research.

Clickers

While ACASI is similar to traditional survey modes in many ways, another new technology currently in use makes respondents an interactive part of the data collection process. **Clickers** are wireless, handheld devices that allow users to instantly register their response to a posed question. They are currently most widely found in classroom settings, where they are typically used as a means of testing what students know—a sort of electronic pop quiz. They are also used to

Respondents may be more apt to disclose information in a T-ACASI survey. *(Shutterstock)*

poll the opinions of the student participants. Clickers are a promising technology partly because the responses registered on the devices are confidential. What they present (instead of individual responses) is the aggregate responses—that is, what percentage of participants selected each answer option. For example, a professor could ask a classroom of students about their views on a proposed smoking ban on campus. Using Clickers, the professor would immediately know what percentage of students in the room support and oppose such a ban. She would not know how each individual student answered the question.

Because of this level of privacy some sociologists believe that they are a very good tool for surveys dealing with sensitive topics. One drawback is that this technology would be appropriate only for quantitative work. Another is that participants must select from a list of preselected and preprogrammed options. Nevertheless, in certain situations and for certain projects, this technology could prove to be extremely useful.

LESSER KNOWN METHODS

Quantitative research is dominated by survey research. Nevertheless, there are some lesser known qualitative methods that can be used in conjunction with survey research or as viable standalone methods. Some are unique to sociology; others have been adapted from other disciplines but are sometimes used in social research. This section will highlight just a few to provide an overview of the different types of research tools and methods that are currently available.

Windshield Survey

A **windshield survey** is a technique in which researchers observe the environment through, you guessed it, the windshield of a vehicle. (It must be noted that the name of this technique is not "full disclosure"—windshield surveys can also be conducted by researchers taking a walk.) Researchers using this technique do not ask people about their beliefs or opinions; they assess situations for themselves. In cases with multiple researchers working on the same study, they do so by employing a measurement tool that ensures everyone on the project is assessing the objects under study in the same way.

Windshield surveys have been frequently used in studies that require assessment of neighborhoods or communities. They can be used, for example, as a means of assessing damage after a natural disaster, such as a tornado. They can also be used to determine levels of accessibility to handicapped citizens or pedestrians.

A windshield survey is often used in conjunction with other research methods. For example, a major city was interested in the percentage of houses under municipal jurisdiction that could be considered "dilapidated." The best way to answer this question would be to survey the residents. In this case a representative sample was acquired and residents were surveyed via telephone on the condition of their homes. Respondents were asked about many things, including the exterior appearance, the condition of the roof, the paint, the windows, and so on.

Assessment of one's own home, however, can be subjective. So to add another layer of validity to the findings, a windshield survey was conducted. Homes that scored high on the dilapidation scale from the telephone survey were listed in a sampling frame. A random sample of homes was taken. Then these homes were visually assessed by researchers. The researchers had a set list of characteristics they were to examine and set criteria for rating those characteristics. This ensured reliability across the research team, meaning that the researchers were using the same scale when rating the homes. The findings from the windshield survey were then compared to the findings from the telephone survey. This allowed for an even more reliable assessment. Comparing the data from the telephone survey to the data from the windshield survey, the researchers found that the results were not significantly different except for comments/responses on the condition of house exteriors: Windshield survey results showed a greater percentage of homes with damaged exteriors than results compiled from the telephone survey showed.

Participatory Action Research

Participatory Action Research (PAR) is similar to participant observation in that the researcher is integrated into the group under study. It differs however in that the researcher's goal is to enact change. The researcher is part of the group and participates in activities designed to change something, generally a perceived injustice. PAR is quite political and very controversial. Researchers engaging in PAR are not objective outsiders but invested insiders. As such, they cannot operate under the typical research norms of objectivity. It is this absence of objectivity that alarms many researchers who believe that PAR crosses the line and is no longer scientific inquiry but simply activism.

An example of PAR can be found in Brett Stoudt's *Brooks Brothers' Blazers & Ivy League: The Use of Participatory Action Research to Examine and Interrupt Privilege in an Elite Private School*. In this study, Stroudt worked with four faculty members and four students at an all boys' school to examine the bullying situation that had been occurring there. Stroudt realized that many power relationships existed within this elite institution, with some students being more privileged than others. Conducting semi-structured interviews with nearly 100 students and 10 faculty and staff members, Stroudt also found that bullying was a major problem at the school: "79% of the students reported hazing/initiations existed to some extent . . . 75% reported fighting/physical violence, 99% reported bullying/intimidation, and 100% reported ridiculing/ teasing existed to some extent." During the study, students at the school were able to communicate on a whole new level by expressing their concerns and opinions that had heretofore remained hidden. Stroudt hoped that his study would help produce major changes in the school by generating a type of bullying reform. Unfortunately the system was so entrenched that change was resisted, although he was successful in establishing new channels of communication with students and staff.

Photoethnography

Photoethnography involves giving research participants a camera so they can take photos of a setting or of people and situations of interest. The participants are then interviewed by the researcher to determine what their photos mean to them and why they are important. Many researchers using different methods include photos in their research articles; photoethnographists use the photographs as a way to solicit information and understanding from the participants. Photoethnography has been used to study many different things, many of them related to oppression or discrimination against low income or disabled people or similar social inequities.

Photoethnography is often used as a tool in PAR. In this context, participants are given cameras and asked to photograph examples of what they view as important in a given cause. In a PAR study focusing on improving living conditions in a community, for example, participants would be asked to go into a designated neighborhood and take pictures of what they viewed as the worst examples of poor living conditions. They would then be interviewed and asked why they chose the specific things they had photographed and what those places, objects or scenes meant to them.

Steven Farough used photoethnography to study a historically privileged group—white men—in his study examining race and masculinity. Farough had each participant take photographs "of phenomena that reminded him of race relations and/or whiteness and things that reminded him of gender relations and/or masculinity." After the participants took the photographs and the pictures were developed, Farough found evidence that the participants viewed race and masculinity in ways that reinforced their privileged status as white men in the United States. For example, one participant took a photo of the high school he had attended and discussed how there was often racial tension because people would hang out with other people from their same racial or ethnic group. When asked about white students he responded that white people "just did their own thing." The discussion revealed that white students typically associated with other white students—a situation that was viewed as normal and unobjectionable whereas the same behavior among members of other racial groups was viewed negatively. When Farough asked the respondent, "But did you get the sense that . . . they [whites] were positioning themselves around being a racial group?" he replied, "No, just hanging out with whom they hung out."

Photoethnography is not a widely used or widely accepted research methodology but it has given some researchers a way to explore social issues in a new way. One interesting (and arguably positive) feature of this method is that it gives study participants (rather than the researcher) the final say in what is important enough to photograph and for what reason.

Autoethnography

Autoethnography (which is not to be confused with ethnography) is another lesser used research methodology. Whereas ethnography is an in-depth qualitative method that relies on participant observation and in-depth interviews, autoethnography focuses on only one person—the writer. Autoethnography is an autobiographical account of the writer's life in which a person's lived experience is explored in depth. The subjective lived experiences are the data.

Lisa Tillmann-Healy used autoethnography to explore the problem of eating disorders in a study entitled "A Secret Life in a Culture of Thinness: Reflections on Body, Food, and Bulimia." In this article, Tillman-Healy describes her own struggle with bulimia, revealing painful details of her battle with bulimia, which began at age fifteen. She recalls, for example, how she believed there was always something "wrong" with her body, a belief that first surfaced when she was 4 years old. She then describes weighing herself at the age of 7, thinking she had cellulite at the age of 10, her first purging episode at age 15, and ending her struggle at age 25. The account is so thorough that the reader feels as though he or she is flipping through the pages of Tillmann-Healy's diary. Such insight allows the reader to understand better how it *feels* to go through bulimia, not just what others *think* being bulimic is like.

Autoethnography differs from most sociological methods in many ways and is very controversial. It is much more literary in style than typical sociological works, reading almost like a novel. It also relies on the author's own experiences. Whereas personal experience is often avoided in sociological work because personal experience is not necessarily indicative of larger processes, it is an essential component of autoethnography. But because of this reliance on personal experience, the method has not gained prominence or widespread acceptance in the field.

SUMMARY

Some methods, such as survey research and interviewing, dominate social research, but there are many others that researchers explore, use, and sometimes rely upon. Some of the lesser known methods have been around for a long time even though they have not been widely used. Still others are the by-products of new technologies. As technology continues to evolve, there is no doubt that the way sociological research is conducted will change as well.

Further Reading

Conrad, Frederick G., and Michael F. Schober. *Envisioning the Survey Interview of the Future*. Hoboken, N.J.: Wiley-Interscience, 2007.

Greene, Jennifer C.. *Mixed Methods in Social Inquiry* . San Francisco, Calif.: Jossey-Bass, 2007.

Muncey, Tessa. *Creating Autoethnographies*. Los Angeles: Sage, 2010.

Parker, Robert Nash, and Emily K. Asencio. *GIS and Spatial Analysis for the Social Sciences: Coding, Mapping and Modeling*. New York: Routledge, 2009.

Stoecker, Randy. *Research Methods for Community Change: A Project-Based Approach*. Thousand Oaks, Calif.: Sage Publications, 2005.

CHAPTER 6

ETHICS IN RESEARCH

The point of conducting any type of research is to discover that which is not yet known. In conducting research we do such things as test hypotheses, and refine and develop theories to explain what we observe. Research, then, is the embodiment of the freedom of inquiry, a fundamental right in all democratic societies. At the same time, sociological research, like research in all the other social and behavioral sciences, involves human beings, their lives, their views, and their experiences. While researchers have the right to conduct research, research subjects have rights too. It is essential that research be designed and implemented so that the rights of human subjects are respected.

A lot of the research conducted by sociologists is essentially innocuous and does not pose any ethical dilemmas. A simple study asking participants about their voting behaviors is not going to pose ethical issues that will need to be addressed. Nor will a study asking people about their views on vegetarianism. Nevertheless some research broaches sensitive topics that raise significant ethical considerations. A study asking people to recount a traumatic experience, for example, can present serious ethical issues. Moreover, the research design itself can lead to ethical dilemmas. There are some general rules that guide ethical research which have been instituted to protect research subjects.

INFAMOUS STUDIES THAT LED TO ETHICAL GUIDELINES
Throughout the history of research there are many egregious examples of unethical behavior. Most of these examples come from the field of medical research;

however, there are several that come from the world of social research. One of the most infamous cases of unethical research in the medical community is the Tuskegee syphilis experiment. This and the other cases discussed here serve to illustrate how ethical oversight in research came about and what guidelines now exist for researchers.

Tuskegee Syphilis Experiment

In the 1930s, during the Great Depression, the United States Public Health Service (PHS) conducted a study on unwitting, poor, African-American men. The stated purpose of the study was to investigate the effects of syphilis on people of different racial backgrounds (most of the research done up to then had been on white people). The participants were offered a free medical exam, free food, and transportation in exchange for participating in the study. They were also offered a "survivors benefit," which meant that their families would receive money for burial expenses when they died. Because of the participants' race and economic background, many had never had a medical exam before, and they certainly did not have money saved for final arrangements, thus making participation in the study very appealing. The PHS also worked with many groups in the community, including churches, to build support for the study and to build credibility. What arguably made the study so credible, however, was that it was affiliated with the Tuskegee Institute, which had an excellent reputation.

Six hundred men enrolled in the study: Examinations showed that 399 had syphilis, 201 did not. The infected subjects were not told that they had syphilis. At the onset of the project, there was no cure for the disease, which had debilitating consequences and could be fatal. The men were placed in treatment and control groups. None of the men received any treatment. The study was supposed to last for six months but it lasted much longer. It went on for forty years. In 1947, it was discovered that penicillin could treat syphilis. The men enrolled in the study were not offered penicillin or informed about this treatment. During WWII, when several of the men enrolled in the draft and it was discovered that they had syphilis, PHS would not allow them to be treated because they were still part of the research study. Many of the men in this study had given syphilis to their wives and partners, which in turn led to many of their children being born with congenital syphilis.

The study was finally stopped in 1972 after news of what was occurring was brought to the media's attention. It remains one of the most heinous examples of unethical research in the history of the United States. The subjects were not informed of the purpose of the study, and deception was certainly not a necessary component. A medical treatment was available to treat the men in the study and this treatment was withheld. There is clearly no ethical gray area in regards to this study. It was unethical. But as you will see, what constitutes unethical research is not always so clear.

Milgram Experiments

Another study involving deception was conducted by psychologist Stanley Milgram. Interested in exploring how it was that people so willingly followed the Nazis during World War II, Milgram designed an experiment to test deference to authority and to ascertain how far people would be willing to proceed in an experiment if they were told to continue.

The experiment worked like this. A subject was brought in and told that he was going to be paired up with another subject. This other subject was actually a member of the research team. The stated purpose of the research was to determine if electric shocks could help people learn word associations. The fake subject (research team member) was in one room, and the real subject was in another. The real subject was directed by a supposed Harvard doctor to administer shocks to the other subject whenever the subject failed to make a correct word association. There were of course no shocks being administered, but the real subject did not know this. Each session began simply enough, and the subjects administered the shocks as they were instructed without much consequence. However as the experiment progressed and the "voltage" increased, the fake subject began yelling for the real subject to stop. He would yell about how he was in pain and how he had a heart condition. Film documentation from the experiment shows the struggle that the real subjects went through during the experiment. By the end of the first set of experiments, 26 of the 40 participants had administered the highest level of electricity possible.

Subjects were debriefed at the conclusion of the session. **Debriefing** is a conversation between an experimenter and a subject that takes place after an experiment is over. In this discussion, the real purpose of the research is explained. Debriefing is done to prevent any long term psychological damage to the person that participated. In this case, the fake subject joined in the debriefing to assure the real subject that no real damage had been done. During the debriefing researchers sometimes explore why the subject participated. In this case, the overarching question was why so many of the subjects continued with the experiment when the person in the other room begged them to stop administering electric shocks. Because over half of the participants administered the highest amount of electricity possible, this experiment provided great insight into the role that authority plays in people's willingness to be obedient, even when they do not feel comfortable complying.

Stanford Prison Experiment

Another experiment highlights how studies can sometimes pose situations that were not anticipated by the researchers. Phillip Zimbardo, a psychology professor at Stanford University, designed an experiment to examine the effects of being a prisoner or prison guard. The participants were all male college students. Of the 75 who applied to participate, 24 were selected. All participants were screened for psychological issues prior to being accepted into the experiment. Participants were also randomly assigned roles—some were prisoners, the others were prison guards.

The "jail" was actually a basement of one of the buildings on Stanford's campus but Zimbardo and his team made sure to make the environment as authentic as possible. On the first day of the experiment, the "prisoners" were "arrested" and brought to the jail. The local police force assisted in this part of the experiment not only by transporting the prisoners but also by "booking" them on charges. All of this was done in an effort to make the situation seem as real as possible. Once in the jail, the student guards and prisoners quickly began behaving as if the situation were real. Guards went as far as to strip search some of the inmates. Prisoners tried to mount an escape, and one went on a hunger strike, resulting in solitary confinement.

The experiment quickly got out of control. Although the experiment was planned to last two weeks, it was stopped on day six. There is footage from the experiment available including the documentary film, *Quiet Rage: The Stanford Prison Experiment*, which Zimbardo wrote.

The Tea Room Trade
A famous sociological research study that has led to widespread discussions about what is ethical and what is not was conducted by Laud Humphreys while he was earning his Ph.D. Humphreys decided he would observe behavior that was occurring at a local park in St. Louis, Missouri. The park where he conducted his study included public restrooms that were well known as places where men engaged in homosexual activity. In his book, Humphreys states that he served as a "watch-queen." That is, he served as a look-out while men would engage in sexual activities. The one restroom had a small patch of woods behind it. The police in the park were often on horseback and could easily look through the windows to see what they were doing. Someone serving as a look-out could alert the others to police presence.

Humphreys never told the men in the park that he was a sociology student or that he was conducting research. Moreover, he did not just observe what was occurring. He also spent time in the park copying down the license plates of the men that were in bathrooms. He eventually took the license plate numbers to a friend who was a campus officer and was given the men's names and addresses. Humphreys then donned a disguise, went to the men's homes, and conducted interviews with them. During these interviews he did not ask about the activities in the park. In fact he never spoke of them. Instead he came to the home under one of his other roles, as a health services surveyor. He asked the men about basic demographics such as age, occupation, and marital status. He also asked them about the quality of their marriages. In all, he interviewed fifty men from the park.

Humphreys found that a majority of the men were married. On the surface they appeared to be upstanding citizens and active in their communities and churches. Many of the men stated that they had happy marriages overall but that there was some marital tension. A common source of this tension was what was perceived as an inadequate amount of sexual relations with their spouses. Much of this was due, it seems, to the high percentage of wives who were Catholic and who practiced abstinence to prevent pregnancies. (Modern birth control was not widely accepted as a viable option by Catholic women in those days because of the church's religious teachings). Overall only 14 percent of the sample was openly homosexual men who identified themselves as a part of the gay community.

Humphreys' findings transformed the way people viewed those who engage in such activities, with most previously assuming that everyone who did so was homosexual (and single). In the end, no one got hurt. No one was "outed" for their behavior in the park. Divorces did not ensue and people were not fired from their jobs as a result of this research. In addition, a lot was learned about how people can lead double lives. The sexual activity took place in a public park, and therefore Humphreys was within his rights to observe it. These facts led some would-be or erstwhile critics to conclude that Humphreys' research was not unethical. Others contend that Humphreys crossed an ethical line, primarily because the men involved did not know that a research study was being conducted. Moreover, by going to the men's homes, Humphreys had invaded their privacy. And finally, if their activities had been made public, there was a risk that their lives may have been severely impacted.

Did the benefits of the research, that is, what was learned, outweigh the potential risks to the participants in these four cases? Could the information have been learned using another method? The debate regarding the last of the four studies continues. What is clear is that studies of this kind would not be allowed today and would certainly be prevented by current safeguards and oversight.

OVERSIGHT

In 1974 the National Commission for the Protection of Human Subjects of Biomedical and Behavioral Research was created. Among other tasks, this commission was responsible for identifying and developing guidelines for researchers conducting human-subject research. The commission's discussions over the course of an initial four-day meeting and subsequent monthly meetings occurring over the next four years were summarized in a document named the **Belmont Report**, which was named for the conference center at the Smithsonian Institution where the commission met.

The Belmont Report presents basic ethical principles and guidelines that researchers must follow when conducting research with human subjects. These ethical principles fall under three general categories: the principles of respect of persons, beneficence, and justice. The report states that respect of persons "incorporates at least two ethical convictions: first, that individuals should be treated as autonomous agents, and second, that persons with diminished autonomy are entitled to protection." The section related to beneficence reads that "persons are treated in an ethical manner not only by respecting their decisions and protecting them from harm, but also by making efforts to secure their well-being." And finally, the section dealing with justice refers to the requirement that costs and benefits are distributed fairly across participants and potential participants.

Although decades old, this document continues to be used in guiding ethical research. **Institutional Review Boards** (IRBs) use this document in developing their own guidelines. IRBs are professional panels that review plans for research that involves human subjects. Most universities, research institutes, and even many community colleges and high schools, now have IRBs. Researchers submit plans for their studies (including proposed questionnaires if necessary) and consent forms to their IRB. IRBs must approve a study before the researcher begins collecting data. IRBs were put in place as a response to many of the studies discussed above, with the purpose of ensuring that research is following the guidelines set forth in the Belmont Report. Their main purpose is to protect human subjects that participate in research.

It is important for all researchers at a college or university (including students) to obtain IRB approval for their work prior to beginning data collection. Having IRB approval protects researchers if there are adverse consequences to human subjects during the research process.

Protecting Subjects and Respondents

There are several general rules that now protect research participants. The first is that the potential benefits of the research must outweigh the potential risks involved in the research design. If a research study is basically risk free, say an anonymous survey on an innocuous topic like media viewing habits, then nearly any benefit, even satisfaction of one's own curiosity, is sufficient. Sociology majors in college often conduct such studies as a means of learning about the process of data collection and analysis. Some of these studies lead to great benefits in the acquisition of new knowledge. More likely though, is that it is only the student who benefits from the process. If a study is very low risk (what is called "less than minimal risk") or entirely risk free, then learning the research process is a legitimate reason to conduct the study.

Some research, especially in the biomedical sciences, can be very risky to subjects. Research that involves trying out new drugs or medical procedures, for example, can carry extreme risks for participants, including death. This type of research, though, still occurs. But in these studies, as in all other studies with potential for adverse effects, the potential benefits must outweigh the risks. Often, the determination of relative risks and rewards in biomedical research is extremely complicated. Suppose one is testing a drug that *might* prevent cancer. How much injury or death could be inflicted in the course of the research before it would be concluded that the risks outweigh the benefits? In all types of research, including biomedical and sociological, if the potential risks outweigh the potential benefits, then the study should not be undertaken.

In most sociological research, the principal **risk to subjects** is the inadvertent disclosure of information gathered on the promise of **confidentiality**. A study that is confidential is one in which the researcher knows the identity of a research participant but promises not to disclose it. Researchers must take measures to maintain confidentiality. These measures can include storing information in secured areas and using pseudonyms in lieu of real names in writings from a qualitative study. In surveys about alcohol or drug use or criminal behavior, the inadvertent disclosure of a participant's responses could result in serious consequences.

In most types of studies, the researcher will be able to identify the respondents and thus confidentiality must be assured. For example, if you are conducting a longitudinal study using a panel of respondents, you will need to locate the same people for follow-up interviews. You will also want to be able to link the respondents' answers from the first questionnaire to their answers from the second questionnaire. To do this and help maintain confidentiality you will need to give everyone a unique identifier, perhaps an identification number. To match the identification numbers to the actual participants you can keep a master list in a separate file. You will need to keep this file secure. It should also be destroyed when the respondents no longer need to be located for further data collection.

Ironically, an interesting example of how far some sociologists will go to protect the anonymity and confidentiality of human research subjects is Laud Humphreys, whose Tea Room Trade studies created so much controversy and sparked so many debates on ethical research. Humphreys took great pains to ensure that the identity of his research subjects would not be disclosed. He kept his notes across a river in another state locked away in a colleague's office.

Sociologists are not provided the same protections under the law as lawyers and medical doctors. There is no sociological equivalent of doctor-patient privilege, and studies that assure confidentiality to participants can come with certain risks to the researchers. In 1991 a sociology graduate student, Rick Scarce, was sent to jail for four months for refusing to turn over interview transcripts that were subpoenaed as part of an investigation of the vandalizing of an animal research laboratory. Scarce had conducted interviews with many people as a part of his research on radical environmental movements. In his defense, Scarce cited the American Sociological Association's professional guidelines, which maintain that researchers are to protect the confidentiality of their research subjects.

One way researchers can avoid such dilemmas is to conduct anonymous studies. In an **anonymous** study, the researcher does not know the identity of the participants. Anonymous studies therefore pose much less potential risk to participants (and researchers). Participants in anonymous studies are instructed not to include their names anywhere to maintain the anonymity of the study. Anonymous studies are ideal when studying topics involving illegal behaviors such as drug use. However, with many research methods, anonymity is simply not an option.

Obtaining Informed Consent

Another integral component of conducting research is obtaining **informed consent**. One of the stipulations that all IRBs require for research involving human subjects is that research cannot begin until participants have given their consent. Not only must prospective subjects consent to participate, but they must also be informed about the study and this information must explain what the study is about, what they will be expected to do, how long it will take to participate, and any risks or benefits. This is typically done in writing although there are exceptions, especially for studies that involve anonymous research. **Implied consent** can be obtained for mail and phone surveys when actual written consent is impossible. That is, consent is implied by the fact that the respondent participates in the research.

Researchers have to tell subjects enough about the research to ensure that subjects are clear as to what they are consenting to. At the same time, you do not want to say so much that you end up creating unnecessary bias in the data. Suppose you were interested in studying the impact of premarital counseling on marriage quality. Telling study participants that the study is testing the hypothesis that people who have received premarital counseling will have fewer problems than those who have not could introduce bias into the study. It would be better to tell participants that the study is about problems that people sometimes have in their marriages. Moreover, you are not required to reveal all of the hypotheses that you may be testing, nor is it advisable to do so because too much information may inadvertently prompt respondents to answer or behave in certain ways, which can defeat the purpose of the research.

To consent to participation, prospective subjects must be competent. People who have deemed mentally incompetent cannot consent to participate in research. There are also special rules for dealing with certain groups of people, including children, pregnant women, prisoners, and the mentally ill. Children are not allowed to provide consent; their parents must provide consent on their behalf. Prisoners are considered a "protected class" in research, meaning that there are separate guidelines for doing research with them.

Although we have discussed the importance of informed consent, there are certain research designs that do lend themselves to informed consent. In some cases, telling participants about the nature of the study beforehand would negate any potential results and would be pointless. Studies that fall into this category necessitate **deception**. If a study cannot be conducted in another way and the benefits outweigh the risks, studies involving deception can be conducted.

One study that involved deception was focused on examining regional differences in how people reacted to threats to honor. In this study the researchers designed experiments to test the Southern culture of honor. The culture of honor is a theory that has been invoked to explain why the South has higher rates of homicide and violence in general as compared to other regions in the country. White, undergraduate male students (half from Northern states, half from Southern states) signed up for an experiment that was explained as a study concerned with the effects of "limited response time conditions on certain facets of human judgment."

The experiment began as participants were walking down a hall to the experiment room. A student working with the experimenters deliberately bumped into a participant and muttered an expletive. This student then walked into a room labeled "Photo lab." While this scenario was in progress, two other members of the research team were sitting in the hallway, seemingly doing homework but actually recording participants' reactions. Participants then went to the experiment room and filled out questionnaires. Once the questionnaires were complete the participants were told that what had occurred in the hallway was an experiment and a meeting between the "bumper" and the participant occurred. The researchers found that students from the South reacted with much more anger to the incident than students from the North. Clearly, the experiment would not have been possible without deception. Because it is difficult to see how any long-term harm could have been inflicted as a result of the study, the deception was probably warranted.

Vulnerable Populations

Some groups of people are considered to be vulnerable populations and are accorded special protection in research situations. Vulnerable populations include prisoners, children, cognitively impaired adults, and pregnant women. Research with participants in these populations can be conducted, but certain safeguards must be in place. When doing research with children, for example, consent must be obtained from a parent or guardian. If the child is older than age seven, he or she must also give consent.

Incentives

A final component in conducting ethical research is that participation must be voluntary and not unduly influenced by the researcher. People must participate in research because they want to, not because they feel that they have to or because they are being coerced to do so. Social service agencies, for example, are forbidden to withhold services to people who do not want to participate. In the classroom, students cannot be told they have to participate in a specific research study as a part of their grade. What is allowed, however, is for researchers to give prospective participants some sort of inducement to participate.

Incentives are inducements or compensation offered to people for participating in a research study. An incentive should be enough to compensate people for their time and effort but not so much that participation stops being voluntary and becomes an unduly influenced agreement to participate. According to the Belmont Report, undue influence occurs "through an offer of excessive, unwarranted, inappropriate, or improper reward or other overture in order to obtain compliance."

In sociological research studies researchers often compensate participants for their time. This compensation can be in the form of food, a gift card, or money. Compensation, however, can be a gray area in terms of undue influence. If a researcher wants to interview high school students for an hour, is it unethical to pay them $5 dollars to participate? What about $20? Or $100? To avoid undue influence, researchers should offer the smallest amount possible to compensate people for their time, but what that amount is varies depending on the project and on the participants. If a research project requires a lot of the participants' time, then incentives may be greater than those offered for participation in a shorter study. Likewise, professionals will probably expect a greater level of compensation than what is offered to college students. There are no set rules for what constitutes an acceptable incentive, and the lines between incentives that induce participation and incentives that overcompensate participation are not always clear and are subject to judgment calls. Thus researchers must take great care in determining if an incentive is appropriate and if so what the incentive should be.

SUMMARY

Throughout history there have been egregious examples of unethical research. There have also been research studies that have posed assorted ethical dilemmas. In response to clearly unethical research, many safeguards have been put in place. In the end, however, it is up to researchers to ensure that research is being conducted in an ethical way. By ensuring that participants give informed consent, that they are voluntarily participating in research, and that confidentiality is being ensured, researchers can design and execute ethical studies. Ethical considerations should always be given the utmost attention in social research.

Further Reading

Humphreys, Laud. *Tearoom Trade: Impersonal Sex in Public Places*. 2nd ed. New York: Aldine Transaction, 1975.

Jones, James H.. *Bad blood: The Tuskegee Syphilis Experiment*. New York: Free Press, 1981.

Milgram, Stanley. *Obedience to Authority: An Experimental View*. New York: Harper Perennial Modern Classics, 2004.

Nisbett, R.E., and D. Cohen. *Culture of Honor: The Psychology of Violence in the South*. Boulder, Colo.: Westview Press, 1996.

Stark, Laura. *Behind Closed Doors: IRBs and the Making of Ethical Research*. Chicago: The University of Chicago Press, 2011.

Zimbardo, Philip G. *The Lucifer Effect: Understanding How Good People Turn Evil*. New York: Random House Trade Paperbacks, 2008.

CHAPTER 7

GATHERING AND MAKING SENSE OF DATA

We have discussed basics of conducting your own research in ethical and systematic ways. This chapter goes into greater detail about how to obtain usable data and what to do with them once you have them. Most, but not all, of the concepts discussed in this chapter apply to quantitative methods. We will begin with measurement.

GATHERING SYSTEMATIC DATA

When you conduct research, you are engaged in measurement. **Measurement** refers to the dimension or the quantity of something. There is certainly nothing intrinsically mysterious about "measurement." We measure things all the time. Consider when we "size up" a situation. In this case we are taking an informal measurement of some situation in which we find ourselves. When we "take the measure" of a person, we are trying to assess his or her moral virtue. In fact, "measurement" is a simple extension of the process of perception. The act of perceiving gives us the most basic example of a measurement. In a basic measure we can record a "1" if a thing is within the perceptual field (that is if we see our particular "thing") and a "0" if it is not. For example, we could sit on a bench in a park and look at every person that walks on the path in front of our bench. If the person is talking on a cell phone we would record a "1"; if not, we record a "0." This is not a very sophisticated measurement, but it is still measurement. The principle difference between "taking the measure" of a person and "measuring" something of research interest is mainly that the former is casual and rather haphazard, whereas in the latter case, we strive to be very precise and systematic.

Reliability and Validity

Before measuring social phenomena, measurement procedures must be accurate. For one thing, they need to be **reliable**. A measure that is reliable will produce the same results when it is repeated. For example, if you were not sick and took your temperature with a thermometer several times in an hour, a reliable thermometer would give you the same temperature reading each time (assuming, of course, that your actual temperature truly was constant). However, if you got very different readings every time, even when your actual temperature did not change, then the thermometer would not be considered reliable at all. Measurement procedures that are not reliable are to be avoided because they may lead to conclusions that are completely wrong.

Measurements must also be **valid**. That is, they must measure what they are intended to measure. So a valid measure of intelligence would measure general intelligence and not something else (say, vocabulary or arithmetic skills). Or consider the measurement of racism. A valid measure would measure only a person's attitudes about race; an invalid measure might measure a person's desire to give a socially desirable answer whether it was that person's "true" attitude or not. Validity is an easy concept to understand but is often difficult to achieve when conducting social research.

There are several different types of measurement validity that must be taken into account. Face validity is the most basic form. **Face validity** refers to how valid a measurement seems at face value. Most reasonable people, for example, would accept that strong agreement with the statement "I hate black people" is a measure of racist attitudes. So we would say that such a measurement has strong "face validity."

A second type is **content validity**. Content validity refers to how fully a concept is measured. Take, for example, the concept of religiosity. How would that be measured? To simply ask people how often they attend a worship service is not sufficient because attendance is just one aspect of being religious (and not necessary the most important). In addition to worship service attendance, one might ask about religious affiliation. That would increase the content validity but still only takes into account organized religion. High content validity would also require questions about religious beliefs, frequency of prayer, the importance of religion in a person's life, and so on. A measure must take into account all dimensions of a concept if it is to have high content validity.

Criterion validity means that the measure does not contradict or conflict with other measures of the same social phenomenon. Do standardized tests of intelligence find basically the same results as the teacher's rating of a student's intelligence? If the standardized test results show that the student has very low intelligence while the student's teachers say that the student is one of the smartest students they have ever taught, the standardized test may not have high criterion validity. A measure with high criterion validity will be strongly related to other measures of the same phenomenon.

Units of Analysis

An important consideration in research design is the unit of analysis. The **unit of analysis** refers to what or whom is being researched. There are five basic types of units of analysis. The first and most common is the individual. If a researcher is interested in gangs, she may decide to interview individual gang members. A second type of unit of analysis would be groups. For instance, our researcher may decide to assess differences between major gangs. In this example, the individual gang members are not of interest; the focus is on the group(s). A specific type of group can also be a unit of analysis in research. This usually includes somewhat formal and organized groups, like workplaces, clubs, or churches. Another specific type of "group" is an aggregate of people that can be found in specific cities and counties, under the same political jurisdictions. These first three units of analysis focus on people. A fourth type is social interaction. This is different from the first three because it does not focus on people but on interactions between and among people. Examples include simple interactions like eye contact or how people greet one another. It might also include more complex interactions, such as homicide. The final common unit of analysis discussed in this chapter is social artifacts. This might seem like something that belongs in the discipline of archeology rather than sociology, but it simply refers to anything that people make and can be used to tell sociologists something about the people who make them and use them. Music videos, websites, drawings, and diary entries are all examples of social artifacts.

It is important to recognize the unit of analysis in research because not doing so can result in errors in conclusions. One such error is called the **ecological fallacy**. This occurs when incorrect assumptions about individuals are made based on findings about the group with which the individual is somehow associated. For example, it might be shown that neighborhoods with more homeless people have higher crime rates, but this does not mean that homeless people are committing lots of crimes. It may only be that neighborhoods with lots of homeless people are also poor neighborhoods and that poverty, not homelessness, drives up the crime rate. Making inferences about individuals based on relationships among aggregates is the ecological fallacy.

Levels of Measurement

Measurement is the process of assigning numbers to units of analysis to capture variable properties of those units. Researchers use four different **levels of**

measurement. The most basic level of measurement is **nominal**, which simply uses names to differentiate between people or things. Nominal variables are sometimes called "categorical variables" because numbers are used to represent names or categories. Consider the numbers you see on the backs of the football team. The quarterback is number 22; the tight end is number 88. All the numbers denote is that the quarterback and the tight end are different players. There is no implication that player 88 is "higher" than player 22, much less four times higher. The numbers are used simply to denote differences not rank order the names or numbers or categories involved. Many variables of sociological interest are inherently nominal.

Biological sex is another example of a nominal variable. We cannot say that males are "higher" or "more" than females. Males and females are just categories of biological sex. The same applies to religious affiliation, ethnicity, and many other human attributes. But consider the concept of "femininity" or "masculinity." Some women are more feminine than other women; some men, for that matter, are more feminine than other men, and even more feminine than some women. So while "sex" is only a question of different categories and thus is nominal, "femininity" is a matter of more or less and is therefore not a nominal variable but something we call an ordinal variable.

At the **ordinal** level of measurement, there is a clear "more and less" aspect to the attributes being measured. Imagine that we have developed a set of questions that generates a 1 to 7 measure of "femininity" where 1 = very low femininity and 7 = very high femininity. This might be as simple as asking people to rate themselves on a 1 to 7 scale of femininity or as complex as asking how much people like or dislike things like "nursing," "babies," or "charades." Now we can definitely speak about more and less feminine. But beware: Although 6 is twice as much as 3, a person who scored as a 6 on our scale cannot be described as twice as "feminine" as a person who scored 3. That is because with ordinal measures the distance between the attributes is not consistent. Although we can say that 2 is more than 1 and 3 is more than 2 in our scale, we cannot say that the distance between 1 and 2, or 2 and 3, is equal. The scale is not based on a constant or recognizable unit.

The next level of measurement is **interval**. If the numbers we assign to the different levels or attributes represent some agreed upon unit, then we have interval level measurement. This is because at this level, the numbers each represent an interval of one constant unit. Examples of variables that are measured at the interval level include temperature, SAT scores, and anything that can be counted: number of friends, dollars of income, years of education. At the interval level of measurement, the distance between numeric levels is consistent. Consider the SAT scores of 1200, 1220, and 1240. There is a 20-point difference between each score—a measurable, consistent, and meaningful difference.

If interval measurement has a nonarbitrary (real) zero, we call it **ratio** level measurement because the ratio of the numbers is meaningful. $100,000 is twice as much income as $50,000, and zero income is meaningful. Ten years of education is half as much as twenty years of education. The ratio that is calculated is mathematically meaningful. For SAT scores however, there is no zero as the minimum score is 200. Therefore SAT scores are measured at interval, not ratio, level.

Operationalization

It is important to distinguish between nominal and operational definitions of terms, concepts or variables. **Operationalization** refers to the process of providing a clear and concise definition that allows for a concept or variable to be measured. A nominal definition is basically the "dictionary" definition of the concept or variable. It defines one concept in terms of other concepts. Thus, a nominal definition of intelligence might be the ability to process information and to reason correctly from premises to a conclusion.

An **operational definition** defines a concept or variable in terms of the operations that will be used to measure that concept. It is the precise specification of the decision rule or rules that will be used to assign numbers to represent the variable properties of a phenomenon. Therefore, an operational definition

Nominal and Operational Definitions

Examples of nominal and operational definitions:

Self-esteem (nominal). The sense of self-worth; the tendency to consider oneself as a valuable or worthwhile human being.

Self-esteem (operational). Sum of "agree" responses to statements like these:

- I think of myself as a worthwhile person.
- I have many positive qualities.

Racial prejudice (nominal). The unwarranted tendency to judge people negatively because of their race.

Racial prejudice (operational). Responses to a series of questions that assess attitudes about race.

- Do you believe that people in your race are naturally smarter than people of other races?
- Do you believe that people in your race are superior to people of other races?

of intelligence might be a person's score on a 25-item test designed to measure information processing or reasoning ability.

It is important to stress that, as the name implies, an operational definition specifies certain operations that will be performed in measurement. It specifies how the concept or variable is going to be measured. A nominal definition of "white racism" might be "the belief that whites are intrinsically superior to members of other races." An operational definition might be based on patterns of responses to a long series of questions about whether a respondent would ever vote for a black person for President, whether it would be acceptable for the respondent's daughter to date a black man, and so on.

Sampling

All empirical social science knowledge, no matter the method of research, is based on sampling from a much larger universe of persons, groups, organizations, ideas, thoughts, feelings, or observations that might have been studied instead. While sampling is a technically complex topic complete with technical language and lots of complicated formulas full of Greek symbols, it is quite an intuitive process. If you have ever tasted a spoonful of soup or chili from a large pot to determine if it was in need of any additional ingredients, then you have sampled. The spoonful is a sample. A generalization about the entire contents of the pot (the population, if you will) is made based on the observations of the spoonful.

Moving from the kitchen to the social world, suppose you are assigned to observe elevator behavior. To do this, you will have to sample elevators, people who use them, interactions among the people who use them, times of the day, days of the week, weeks of the year, and so on. It is impossible to proceed in any other way. So you pick one elevator (a small sample, but still a sample) in one building (another small, probably unrepresentative sample) on one convenient day and time (a sample of all the days and times when you might have made your observations), observe what there is to observe, and then—if you take your methods seriously—you wonder if you would get the same results or observe the same patterns on other elevators, in other buildings, or at other times. You wonder, in research language, about the external validity—the generalizability—of your sample.

Before delving deeper into the concept of sampling and different types of samples, there are some terms that need to be understood. The first is **population**. The population is the complete list of elements that the sample will be derived from. In a survey of adults living in the United States, the population is every adult in the United States. If the research project goal is to study the experiences of nurses in a particular hospital, then all of the nurses in that hospital comprise the population. The list of all of the elements in the population is called the **sampling frame**. If a researcher wants to draw a sample of students at a particular university, then the sampling frame would be a complete list of all of the current students. It is from this sampling frame that the actual sample will be drawn.

A **census**, by definition, collects data from all members of a population. The United States conducts a census every decade in which the goal is to survey every resident of the country. While it is certainly true that not everyone is included in the final census, the U.S. Census Bureau strives for this goal. Many measures are put into place to achieve the highest participation rate possible. The U.S. Census aside, for most research projects, surveying each and every person of interest is simply not a viable option. In such cases, sampling comes to the rescue.

Given that the need to sample (times, people, experiences, questions, whatever) is inevitable and omnipresent, the question is not *whether* you sample but *how* you sample. Here the choice is between something formal and systematic, which means that the resulting observations have useful statistical properties; or something informal and haphazard, which means that the resulting observations have no useful statistical properties at all. There is, of course, a third alternative, by far the worst of all: You sample with intentional or unintentional bias, which ensures that the resulting observations are much worse than simply useless and can become positively dangerous. Most people, once they think about it, have no trouble deciding that something formal, systematic, and therefore statistically useful is vastly preferable to every known alternative.

If a sample is to be accurate, the sampling frame must be complete. If it is not, the sample could be biased. A biased sample can have serious consequences in terms of the validity of results from a research study. Consider this real example: The magazine *Literary Digest* confidently predicted a victory for Thomas Dewey over Harry Truman in the 1948 presidential election based on a survey magazine staff conducted. The sample used consisted of the readership of *Literary Digest*. This sample was not a representative sampling of the voting population as a whole and, of course, the results were incorrect.

Although there are many ways to obtain biased samples, there is only one way to end up with unbiased samples, and that is when chance and chance alone dictates which observations are in the sample and which are not. Let these decisions be made by anything other than chance, and bias can result. This is the underlying concept behind probability sampling.

Probability Sample

Whether you realize it or not, you are very familiar with probability. Before testing that chili we are using for illustrative purposes, you have to make sure the pot is thoroughly stirred. Probability sampling is how human populations are "thoroughly stirred." You stir the pot of chili to make sure all the ingredients are evenly distributed throughout the pot. The sampling equivalent is to make sure that every element in the population has a known, calculable probability of being in the sample. True probability samples are the most desirable type of samples. What makes them so special is that findings based on these samples can generalize to a larger population. **Generalizability** is the ability to take the findings that were discovered from the sample and apply them to the larger population that the sample was drawn from.

Simple random sample

The most straightforward type of sample has a somewhat misleading name. It is called a **simple random sample**. A simple random sample is one in which every member of the population of interest has an equal chance of being selected for the sample. Its premise is easily understood when thinking of a standard die. When someone rolls a die, the numbers 1–6 each have an equal chance of landing on top. The same is true in a simple random sample, even if there are 50,000 units in the population of interest. The simple random sample requires that a complete list of the population exists to form the sampling frame.

To illustrate how the simple random sample works let's suppose that a researcher wants to conduct a study of college professors at one university. Let's say there are 900 professors. A list of this population certainly exists, so the researcher writes each name on a separate slip of paper. All of the slips of paper are put in a box and shaken. Then the researcher pulls the number of slips of paper needed to complete the sample.

The researcher could have also used a random number table or random number generator to select the sample. In this case the list of the professors would be numbered sequentially from 1 to 900. Using a random number table the researcher would start by selecting 3 numbers in a row. Any number above 900 would be thrown out (say 986) and the next three numbers would be selected. This is very effective but quite tedious. Today there are random number generators available on the Internet. With these generators you input the range (for us it would be 1–900) and input how many random numbers you need.

Nonprobability Sampling

Although probability samples are ideal as they allow for findings to generalize, oftentimes they are not possible to obtain. They can also be extremely expensive, time consuming, and technically complex. Researchers conducting studies without the benefit of funding may not even be able to consider the possibility of obtaining a probability sample. If a probability sample is not possible, it does not mean that research should not be conducted. It does, however, mean that generalizing the results beyond the sample can be quite problematic. This is because in a nonprobability sample every element in a population does not have an equal chance of being selected. It is therefore quite possible that those in the sample differ from those not in the sample in important ways. A lot has been learned through research that has used non-probability samples, but generalizing beyond the sample can be hazardous and should be avoided.

Convenience sample

The least desirable type of nonprobability sample is a convenience sample. A **convenience sample** consists of people that are simply available. They are not randomly selected. Everyone in the population did not have an equal chance of being sampled. Convenience samples are generally used when there is no other choice. Oftentimes, lack of resources (time, money, and researchers) precludes a random sample from being drawn. At other times, no list of the population is available. The biggest concern with research done using a convenience sample is that the findings do not generalize to anything. Nevertheless, often for the reasons mentioned above, much research is conducted using convenience samples. Although the results cannot generalize, knowledge can still be acquired and the social world can be better understood.

Let's suppose that a researcher has decided to conduct a study with a sample of college students at a particular university and that the subject of interest is perceptions about safety on campus. A list of the population does exist. The researcher could acquire a list of all of the students registered at the university in a particular term, randomly select students, and contact them to participate in the study. However, this would require a lot of resources that the researcher may not have. Instead of scrapping the project, the researcher decides to use a convenience sample.

The researcher may go into large classrooms in lecture halls and pass out pen and paper surveys. The only students eligible to be in the sample would be the students that were in the certain classes that the researcher chose and happened to be attending those classes on the day that she passed out the survey. A lot of data can be collected very quickly with this method and while it may not be generalizable to all students at the college, we can still learn something about the topic. Using a convenience sample in and of itself is not problematic; attempting to generalize the findings from a study employing a convenience sample to a larger population is.

A convenience sample does not have to take place on a campus. A researcher might go to a public place, like a library, and ask people to take a survey. Again, the only people eligible to participate would be people that are in the library during the time the researcher is there. Beyond that, people that go to the public library may be different from those that do not go to the library, in important ways. Some provisions can be put into place to make a convenience sample more rigorous. These include purposive samples and quota samples, which are explained in this chapter.

Types of Samples

There are many other kinds of samples, including stratified probability samples and systematic samples. Two other kinds of nonprobability samples are purposive and quota samples.

- A **stratified sample** divides the population into strata on the basis of some variable of interest and then samples each stratum separately. For example, a study may be interested in comparing white students to minority students on a campus where white students outnumber minority students eight to one. A simple random sample would produce too few minority students to sustain the comparison. So divide the sample into two strata: white students in one stratum and minority students in the other; then oversample the minority student stratum and undersample the white student stratum. The result is a sample that allows for efficient comparisons between white and minority students.
- A **systematic sample** is a random sample in which every nth case is selected. This can be a very practical type of sample. Imagine you are asked to conduct a study that involves analyzing data about clients from a social service agency. The agency has all of the client files in file cabinets in an office. You could number every single file and then take a random sample. You would then need to go back and pull all of the files that correspond to the numbers in the sample. Or you could conduct a systematic sample. In this case you would pull every 5th or every 8th file, whatever your n ends up being. This is much less tedious and still results in a probability sample. Now if you just pulled all of the files from two drawers in one of the file cabinets, it would not be a probability sample as only people that have files in those two drawers could have been selected. But if you take every nth case, the entire population is involved. A systematic sample should not be used when there is some pattern present in the sampling frame—if, for example, files were ordered (for some reason) by length of time people were clients in the agency.
- A **purposive sample** is one in which sample members are selected to fulfill the purpose of a study. If you want to study college students that have chosen to major in sociology, you would actively go seek people

Snowball sampling

Snowball sampling is a technique where people who are part of a sample are asked to help the researcher by recruiting other people to participate in the study. Snowball samples are typically, but not always, used in quali-

that you know fit this criterion. If you were using a regular convenience sample and surveyed 300 students, there is a chance that none of the people in your sample would be sociology majors. Although the sample is still not a probability sample, you are assured that your sample consists of people that meet the criterion you are interested in. For another example, let's say you are interested in surveying college athletes. Clearly you should start by sampling at a college. From there you could just survey in classrooms or on campus, but this could result in no athletes ending up in your sample. If you are interested in athletes, it would be much more productive to survey in a place where you know your sample will consist of people that possess the characteristic you are interested in, such as a study hall for athletes run by the athletics department.

- A **quota sample** is a sample in which a certain number of sample elements need to be in each predetermined category. This technique is used to correct for the biggest problem with convenience sampling: namely that there is no control in place to make sure the sample is similar to the larger population of interest. It is also essential when using a quota sample that you know general information about the larger population. Typically quota samples will recruit participants on one or two characteristics that are of particular interest, for example, gender and approximate age. Such a sample will "match" known population distribution on these two variables but may not "match" on any other characteristics that might be important. Let's say you want to do a study comparing differences in student opinions about a pending university policy change. You are particularly interested in whether class standing impacts these opinions. Therefore you decide to do a quota sample so your sample will reflect the breakdown of class levels within the university. You go to the university's Website and determine that the university's undergraduate population comprises 30 percent freshmen, 30 percent sophomores, 20 percent juniors, and 20 percent seniors. You want to take a sample of 1,000 students. Instead of just going into classes and hope that you get a good mix of students, you decide to set quotas. For a sample of 1,000, that might break down to 300 freshmen, 300 sophomores, 200 juniors, and 200 seniors.

tative work and used when finding people that meet certain criteria may be challenging. The process is called snowball sampling because the sample gets bigger over time, just as a snowball rolling down a hill does. Snowball sampling can also help in acquiring participants in a study that may focus

Snowball Sampling

Kelly Worthen, an undergraduate sociology student, designed a research project studying the differences in modes of communication of different generations (Baby Boom, Generation X, and Generation Y). The study consisted of a Web based survey designed to elicit people's preferred modes of communication (face-to-face, text messaging, telephone, etc.) and their opinions on changing technology. As an undergraduate student, finding Generation Y participants was not a challenge. But to find members of the other generations, he used snowball sampling. Generation Y participants were asked to forward the survey link to younger and older people in their families or circles of friends and colleagues. This allowed for a sample consisting of all three generations to be secured.

on sensitive topics or might include people that have unique characteristics or participate in rare groups. It is also an effective way to find participants that are engaged in illegal behavior. Snowball sampling takes advantage of people's social networks and people who can help persuade others that a study is legitimate.

Let's suppose a researcher wants to study computer hackers. The researcher knows two people that engage in this activity. He asks both of them to participate in the research and they agree. He then asks them if they can refer other hackers to participate in the study. They each know two more people that are hackers. So the researcher then contacts the referrals. The researcher continues this process until he finds enough people or is no longer successful in finding new participants.

Although this method of sampling can be invaluable in garnering participants who may otherwise be difficult to locate, there are some disadvantages. One is that finding enough participants that meet the criteria for a rare topic of interest can be difficult. Secondly, when relying on an initial contact, the referrals may not have a large enough circle of people that possess the necessary characteristic, so your referrals can quickly end up being people you have already asked. Another concern is that because your sample will consist of people connected through an initial contact, they may differ substantially from members of the group as a whole.

MAKING SENSE OF DATA

Statistics is a field of study within mathematics that deals with the collection, analysis, and interpretation of quantitative data. Statistics also refers to the actual tests that are performed in analyses of data. Statistics are vital in quantitative sociological research. Although a full discussion of statistics is outside the scope of this book, this section will present the basics to help you understand how sociologists make sense of the data they collect.

Distribution of the Data

Data refers to the information collected in a research study that is going to be analyzed. Whereas in qualitative work we typically code data to assess themes, in quantitative work we usually want to produce statistical findings: how much, how many, where located, correlated with what. Consider a variable that is near and dear to the hearts of any student: the Grade Point Average. Over time, a student's grades are a collection of As, Bs, Cs, and so on (note that these grades are themselves measurements—one hopes that they are valid and reliable measures!). This collection of grades can be arranged into a **frequency distribution** that shows the number of As earned, Bs earned, and so on. Perhaps the frequency distribution for one student would be:

A 7
B 9
C 5
D 2
F 0

Two things can be observed about this distribution: First, it has an average or what statisticians call a **central tendency**; secondly, there is some **dispersion** of scores or grades above and below that average. Dispersion refers to how the data points are scattered around a certain value, like the mean or the median. In the present case, we might assign an A 4 points, a B 3 points, and so on, and we could then calculate a grade point **average** for this particular student thusly:

$4 \times 7 = 28$
$3 \times 9 = 27$
$2 \times 5 = 10$
$1 \times 2 = 2$
$0 \times 0 = 0$

If we add up the products, we get $28 + 27 + 10 + 2 + 0 = 67$, and if we divide that sum by the number of grades ($7 + 9 + 5 + 2 = 23$), we get this student's grade point average: $67/23 = 2.91$. This student, in other words, averages just short of a B in all the courses represented in the table, which makes sense because the student has nine Bs, seven grades higher than B, and seven grades lower than B.

Consider another student whose 23 grades are distributed as follows:

A   0
B   22
C   0
D   1
F   0

This student has exactly the same grade point average as our first student (67 total points, 23 grades, GPA = 2.91) but obviously the two grade distributions are not the same. The first student has some As, more Bs, a few Cs, and so on; the second student gets Bs in virtually every course taken (and one D). So while the two distributions have the same average or central tendency, the second distribution shows a lot less dispersion of scores around the average.

Oftentimes, we are less interested in how a variable is distributed than in how one variable is related to another. Suppose, for example, that we were not interested in individual GPAs but whether females on average have better grades than males. To show a relationship, we would calculate an average GPA for all the females (in a class or a school or even a state), an average GPA for all the males, and then compare the two averages. There are lots of fancy ways to express the degree of statistical correlation between two factors, but the comparison of group averages is one intuitively obvious and appealing way to do so.

Measures of Central Tendency

As the previous discussion implies, measures of central tendency are descriptive statistics that describe an average or typical value for a frequency distribution. In the above example, we calculated a mean. **Mean** is simply another word for average. To calculate the mean you simply add up all of the responses and then divide by the number of responses. In our example, we calculated a mean for grade point average by assigning a number to each letter grade (A = 4, B = 3, C = 2, D = 1, F = 0), then added up the numbers assigned to the grades and then divided this by the number of grades. We could have also calculated an average (or mean) height for students in a class, or a mean weight for players on the football team, or the mean salary of teachers, and so on. In each case, we add up the values of the observations and divide by the number of observations to get the arithmetic mean or average.

There are two other commonly used measures of central tendency for a frequency distribution. One of these is the median. The **median** refers to the *midpoint* (or the middle value) of the distribution of data. Half of the data points fall above the median and the other half below in a distribution. Thus in our example, the median is B, or its numeric equivalent, 3.

Finally the **mode** is the *most common* category in the distribution. In the case of the first student above, the mode (or modal grade) is B, since that student had more Bs than As, Cs, Ds, or Fs. In this example, the median and mode are the same, but this is not always the case.

Variables

A **variable** is anything that can *vary*, or take on different values. In the examples we have been using, grades are a variable because different students receive different grades and we can characterize students according to the grades they have received. That is one variable (one way that students may vary). We could also construct a variable "class standing" (freshmen, sophomores, juniors, seniors.) And once you think about it, there are many additional variables we might use to characterize students: height, political orientations, self-esteem, parents' income, and so on.

Simply put, variables *vary*. They take on different values for different people (or other objects). If they do not vary, they are called **constants**. We are not interested in constants because if something is constant then there is nothing for us to study. For example, in a study of sorority members, all of the sorority members will be female. Therefore "gender" in this study is a constant. We cannot analyze differences in sorority experiences based on gender because gender in this case does not vary. In this instance it would be obvious to us at the beginning of the study that gender would be a constant. Sometimes a constant is not so obvious. For example, we could do a study in a high school classroom and one of our variables of interest might be age. Once we collect our data we may realize that everyone is the same age. Age then would no longer be a variable, it would be a constant.

There are two main types of variables in research: independent and dependent. **Independent variables** are variables in which the values are already set. They do not depend on anything. These are often demographic variables. Variables such as gender, race, and age will be set; they will not depend on other factors. **Dependent variables** are affected by the independent variables. For example, in an analysis examining the impact of gender in support for gun control, gender would be the independent variable and support for gun control would be the dependent variable. A person's gender will not change regardless of his or her views on gun control, or any other social issue for that matter. However, views on gun control may be different for men than for women. People's opinions on social issues are impacted by a myriad of variable characteristics: gender, race, socioeconomic status, education, religious affiliation, and so forth. This leads us to a third type of variable that is important to consider in quantitative research: the intervening (or control) variable.

Intervening variables are variables that may have an impact on the relationship between independent and dependent variables. They are sometimes called "control" variables because when we do statistical analysis, they can be included and thus "controlled for." A classic example of an intervening variable can be found in Emile Durkheim's study of suicide. Durkheim found in his analysis that suicide rates were lower among married people than single people. There was, however, an intervening variable that was actually responsible for the association that was being observed—namely the level of social integration (how connected people are to others). The level of social integration was higher among married people, and it was this degree of integration, and not marital status per se (it just so happened that married people were more integrated than unmarried people), that was actually the cause of their lower levels of suicide.

If something else might be affecting your dependent variable, you need to measure it if at all possible—that way you can control for it. But how do you know what the relevant intervening variables might be? The key way researchers identify intervening variables (and independent variables) is by conducting an extensive literature review. It is almost certain that others have thought about and tested variables that are possibly connected to your topic. Often, theory will also suggest critical intervening variables.

It is the relationship between your independent variables and the dependent variable that your analysis will seek to understand and it is this analysis that will lead you to your conclusion. Therefore it is very important that you make sure that you gather data on all of the variables that may potentially be important.

Correlations

A **correlation** between an independent and a dependent variable means that there is a relationship between them. To return to our earlier example, if the average GPA of girls in a middle school is higher than the average GPA of the boys, we say that gender and GPA are correlated. In statistics, positive correlations are relationships that move in the same direction. For example, we know that as education increases, so too does income. Thus there is a **positive correlation** between education and income. A **negative correlation** is one in which the variables move in opposite directions. For example, as age increases, health typically declines.

Causation

In sociological research we are often interested not only in investigating a correlation between an independent variable and dependent variable, but **causality**, or cause and effect. There are three criteria that must be present to establish causality:

1. The independent and dependent variables must be correlated.
2. The correct time order must be established.
3. The possibility of a spurious relationship must be ruled out.

Criteria 2 and 3 can be problematic in sociological research. Whereas time order can easily be established in longitudinal studies, it can be much more difficult to determine when data come from cross-sectional research.

Likewise, ruling out all other possible explanations for the relationship can be extremely problematic. Sometimes causation can be apparent but is false. The observed causal relationship can actually be explained by a third variable. When this occurs the relationship between the independent and dependent variable is said to be a **spurious** relationship. If girls have higher GPAs because they study more hours than boys, then the relationship between gender and GPA would be described as spurious because what really matters is not your gender but how many hours spent studying. Experiments, which are discussed in detail in Chapter 2, can establish time order and rule out spurious relationships, however, they are rarely an appropriate research method for the issues that sociologists are most interested in.

Validity

We have already discussed validity as it relates to measurement. Validity is also a concern of the overall research design. Generally there are two forms of validity that fall under this heading: internal and external. **Internal validity** means you can assert that your outcome is a result of changes in the dependent variable in a study where a causal relationship is being sought. **External validity** generally means that the results of the study are generalizable to the larger population. Issues of internal validity can be controlled through the design of a study; however there are several major potential threats to internal validity of nonexperimental designs. But these are beyond the scope of the present discussion.

Errors in Reasoning

Errors in reasoning occur when people make unwarranted inferences from the data they have gathered. Learning about some common errors in reasoning will help you to spot weak points in arguments. The following are the most common errors in reasoning:

Overgeneralization

In research, **overgeneralization** refers to making sweeping conclusions based on limited observations. Overgeneralization can, and does, occur in daily life. Overgeneralization is strongly related to stereotypes. In a research setting, overgeneralization can mean taking the findings of one study and applying them to larger or different groups. For example, let's say you conduct a survey of 100 fraternity members at a small liberal arts college. One of your findings is that the majority of these fraternity members think having sex with a woman who has had too much to drink is acceptable behavior. An overgeneralization would be to infer that all men, all college men, or even all the men at this small liberal arts college think likewise. They might very well think so, but your finding is not evidence that they do.

Selective Observation

In **selective observation**, you purposefully seek out observations that confirm your preexisting beliefs or opinions, or even more insidiously, make mental notes only of observations that are consistent with those preexisting beliefs. If I believe that men are more likely to speed than women, I am apt to notice men who are driving fast and women who are observing the speed limit. Slow male drivers and fast female drivers may not be noticed. Men who believe that all blondes are dumb remember the dumb things blondes say and overlook the equally stupid things said by brunettes and redheads (not to mention the stupid things their male friends say!).

Illogical Reasoning

Illogical reasoning means exactly what you would guess. Sometimes it can be reasoning that is completely ludicrous, but more commonly it refers to research conclusions that are not empirically justified. A very common example is reasoning from correlation to cause in precisely the wrong direction. Research shows that successful organizations pay higher salaries and floundering organizations pay lower salaries. Would you therefore recommend to a CEO of a company about to go under that he should raise everyone's salary immediately?

SUMMARY

Oftentimes lay people may think that all sociologists do to conduct research is watch what is going on around them. This chapter clearly shows that this is not the case. To be able to make claims about the social world, the findings must be based on scientifically rigorous research, whether quantitative or qualitative.

Further Reading

Healey, Joseph. *The Essentials of Statistics*. 2nd ed. Belmont, Calif.: Wadsworth, 2010.

Miller, Delbert C., and Neil J. Salkind. *Handbook of Research Design and Social Measurement*. 6th ed. Thousand Oaks, Calif.: Sage Publications, 2002.

CHAPTER 8

RESEARCH DESIGN

Now that you know the basics of qualitative and quantitative research you might wonder how you would really go about conducting a study of your own. Indeed, conducting your own research can be the most fascinating part of being a sociologist. This chapter serves as a "how-to" guide for conducting research. Some of the issues relevant to each of the major methods presented throughout this volume will be discussed.

Research often follows a certain structure. This chapter will guide you through the typical research design used by sociologists conducting their own research. Following this design can be exceptionally helpful to young sociologists just learning how to conduct research. The design consists of developing a topic and research question, reviewing the literature, incorporating a theoretical orientation, explaining the methodology and sample acquisition plan, developing hypotheses to test, analyzing the data, reaching conclusions, and finally, documenting the process and findings for a broader audience.

Qualitative projects often deviate from this design. As you will recall, a lot of qualitative work is inductive in nature meaning that researchers will begin with data collection, which will lead to theory formulation at the conclusion of the research. This chapter will offer some advice about how you might go about conducting a quantitative research project. How a qualitative project study on the same topic might be conducted will also be discussed so you can get a better feel for how these two general methods differ in practice.

STEPS IN THE RESEARCH PROCESS
Step 1: Deciding on a Research Topic
The first step in designing a research study (whether quantitative or qualitative) is deciding on a research topic. In applied work the question may be provided for you by the client (e.g., the question may be: Are (clean) needle exchange programs effective in reducing HIV infections among drug users?). If conducting a study for your own research project, however, the choice of topic can be completely up to you. College students majoring in sociology are sometimes asked to design their own research studies as a part of their coursework. Students are often very excited at the chance to pick their own topic as a change from being told what to write about. Some know instantly what they want to research, maybe a subject that has been fascinating them for a long time. Or they may work in an environment that has led to the development of some research questions. In thinking about what topic to study, one of my undergraduate students remembered that she spends several hours per week volunteering. She often volunteers with the same people and decided that because volunteering was such an important part of her life and had also touched the lives of many of her friends, she could develop a sociological study that focused on volunteerism.

But because sociology is concerned with the social world, choosing a topic is not quite as easy as it sounds. The number of topics is virtually limitless. Oftentimes, students are completely overwhelmed at the thought of choosing a topic. Where to start? There are so many possible topics! Because of this, I encourage students to take a few days to really pay attention to the world around them—and to look at the world in a sociological way. What do they find interesting? Intriguing? What do they see that causes them to question what is going on? I also encourage students to become informed about current events. Doing so can lead to some great studies that examine people's reactions, opinions, and perceptions of current events.

Step 2: Developing the Research Question
Once a general research topic has been selected, the researcher continues to narrow the topic and eventually forms the topic into a research question. A **research question** is the question that the study will attempt to answer. The research question will guide the entire study and help the researcher stay focused. The student mentioned earlier had decided to study volunteerism. This is a very broad topic, so the next step is to take this general topic, narrow it down, and form it into a researchable question. A good research question is clear and focused; it is not vague or too broad. Some questions may not be answerable with limited resources, and this makes them unsuitable. In the end a good research question is one that is do-able.

The following questions related to the broad concept of volunteerism are researchable and focused. Each of them would make an excellent research question:

- What motivates college students to volunteer?
- What are the demographic characteristics of college students who volunteer?
- How do paid staff members and volunteers interact in an agency?
- Do clients in an agency think that the volunteers really care about them?

The list of potential research questions for any particular topic could continue for several pages, but you probably get the idea. There are many different things that can be explored in any topic.

In our case the student decided that given the resources she had available the research question for her study would be "What motivates college students to volunteer?" Already knowing what motivates her to volunteer, she will now be able to study the main reasons many other students volunteer.

When trying to select a research topic or develop a research question, it is not always necessary to find a gap, or a topic no one else has explored. A researcher can design a study that will be the same as a study someone else has previously conducted. The main difference will be the specific people involved in the research. This type of study is called a **replication study**. Replication studies are important because they can corroborate that the findings in a previous study were not a fluke, or that the findings hold across different groups of people or in different circumstances. Something will not (or should not) be accepted as a truism in society on the basis of one study. Thus replication is extremely important in building scientific knowledge. For example, a study conducted at one university may find that students overall hold very negative views towards military service. Is this finding true of all students at all universities? Multiple studies, at different universities that vary in size, student composition, and location would be necessary to determine if this were indeed the case. When conducting a literature review you may come across replication studies that produced different findings from the original study, therefore opening the door for more research on the same topic.

A well-developed research question guides the researcher throughout the project and toward using certain research methods. Some questions are better suited for quantitative methods (What are the demographic characteristics of college students who volunteer?) whereas others may be better addressed through qualitative methods (How do paid staff members and volunteers interact in an agency?). Thus, your research question should always guide selection of method, not vice versa.

Step 3: Researching the Topic

Don't reinvent the wheel. Chances are, others have studied the topic you are interested in. So your next task is to conduct a review of related literature. But the task of organizing all those published works can be daunting! One of the best strategies at this point is to construct an annotated bibliography. An **annotated bibliography** is a list of summaries of articles on a particular topic. Typically an annotated bibliography entry will begin with a citation to the work. The entry itself will consist of one to two paragraphs that describe the study (paraphrased from the article). The entry may also include additional information, such as a note on limitations in the study or a statement about why the article is useful to the present research study. You should always write these entries in your own words unless there is quotation that you know you will use when you write your research paper. In these cases, always clearly mark the passage in quotation marks and include page numbers for later reference. The annotated bibliography can be a great way to begin writing a literature review, which is the next task.

A **literature review** is an essay that discusses previous research and studies on a particular research topic. The literature review is important because it allows the researcher to understand what is already known about a topic. The literature review will show a researcher previous findings on a particular topic and will also show what methods have been used in the past to conduct the studies on this topic. It will also show the researcher what is not known. This is important because identifying the "gaps in the literature" can help guide new research studies or refine your question.

A review of the literature employs two important concepts: tradition and authority. **Tradition** in this sense refers to the written knowledge that has been published to date. It is from this tradition that one derives hypotheses, assesses the credibility of differing empirical claims, and "locates" one's own research within a particular school of thought within sociology. In one prominent view of science, science progresses according to the consensus of a community of scholars; today's "consensus" is tomorrow's scientific "tradition."

Authority refers to those scholars that have become recognized as experts on certain topics or in specific areas of study. Within nearly every subfield there are authorities who are well recognized for conducting important studies that have significantly contributed to the accumulation of knowledge. Reading their works is often vital in understanding the state of knowledge within an area of study.

Both tradition and authority are important in building scientific knowledge. However, there is a fine line between building on the works of others and accepting what has been presented without question. While tradition and authority are important, for any scientific field of inquiry to be able to progress (sociology included), innovative thinking and active questioning of what has been presented by others is required. You should appeal to reason and evidence, not tradition and authority, to establish the validity of claims and propositions.

Most of the literature cited in reviews comes from academic journals. Academic journals are periodicals where scholarly research is presented. All disciplines have academic journals that publish work relevant to their field of study; in sociology there are hundreds. Some have a very wide focus while others specialize in publishing works relevant to certain subfields. Articles in academic journals are usually **peer reviewed**, meaning they have been vetted by experts in the field. The peer-review system is the basis for the publication of all scientific research and ensures that published work is of the highest quality. Thus, it is always best to use peer-reviewed journals when conducting your literature review. Academic journal articles are available in electronic databases that allow researchers to easily locate literature for their research. Articles typically list keywords to assist in this process. A study that explores motivations for volunteering among college students in the United States, for example, may use keywords such as "volunteerism," "motivation," and "college students." An important note: If you are having troubling finding previous literature, it would be prudent to ask why. Perhaps it is not researchable? Perhaps it's one that's really not sociologically important or interesting. For example, who cares whether and why some people

Literature Search Process

Undergraduate student Marie Gualtieri knew that she wanted to study women and body image. Her interest specifically was to examine women's perceptions of "real women" in print advertisements, with a specific focus on the Dove Campaign for Real Beauty. She began searching literature databases using the keywords "Women" and "Print Advertisements." This led to a few articles that were pertinent to her study. (Most articles list keywords that suggest categories under which they might be listed.) Marie looked at all of the keywords listed in the articles she found. Keywords included "Magazines," "Perceptions," "Internalization," "Thin Ideals," and "Self-objectification." While Marie would probably have thought to search under the term "Magazine," a term such as "thin ideals" may not have occurred to her, thus highlighting the importance of reading the keywords listed under relevant articles. By using different combinations of each of the keywords, she was able to locate more articles about her topic. Because she found a diverse group of articles about her general topic, she was able to find an area of the research that had not been considered yet, which helped her to narrow her topic's focus.

pick their noses in public? More than likely, failure to locate other studies on your topic is the result of narrowing your search too much.

Writing literature reviews can be challenging for beginners because reviews are quite different from most other types of writing. They involve the coherent synthesis of the works of others. It is not enough to summarize each study—you must also be able to integrate the works in the literature review as a whole, often organizing paragraphs around themes or topics rather than describing individual studies. Moreover there are technical and scholarly rules to follow. For example, whenever the work of another researcher is being discussed, the literature review must include a citation. A **citation** provides a reference to the source of the information. If works of others are presented without citations, it is a form of plagiarism. **Plagiarism** is the theft of written intellectual thought. It is to be avoided at all costs. Plagiarism can result in severe academic and professional consequences, including expulsion from school or termination from a job.

When taking notes from other sources, it is best to put them in your own words. If you quote directly from the source, however, make sure you have the quoted material in quotation marks in your notes and that you record the page number where the quote originally appeared. You want to limit your use of direct quotations. If you can paraphrase the material, do so! Quotations should be reserved only for thoughts that are expressed in such a way that to paraphrase them would be to lose the impact. As long as the entries have been written in your own words, the risk of plagiarizing another's work is virtually eliminated. It is important to clarify though that a researcher can plagiarize another researcher's work even if the material has not been copied verbatim. Substituting a few words here and there is not enough. As a researcher, you must reword others' work in words and phrases that are clearly different from the original text and give the original researcher credit for the work in the form of a citation.

Step 4: Developing a Theoretical Orientation

It can often be challenging for students to find a theoretical grounding for their own study (particularly if they are not yet educated on social theory). But making sense of findings we uncover in our research in a theoretical way is the work of sociologists. Oftentimes, when conducting a literature review, students will find that studies clearly discuss their theoretical grounding and thus expose students to theories that can help explain the social phenomenon in question on a larger scale. In some areas of study, however, many articles will be **atheoretical** or lacking a theoretical grounding. For example, sociological research focusing on drug abuse has often been deemed atheoretical. And in fact many of the articles in this area support this idea. Nonetheless a search of "drug abuse" and "theory" in a database will quickly reveal that there are many theories that have been developed about or applied to this social phenomenon. Thus, although theory may not be obvious at the onset, making an effort to seek out and explore theories that have been or might be applied to your particular topic can help you see your research from a better perspective and in a larger context.

In the example on volunteerism that we have been using, a review of the literature revealed that many different theories have been used to explain people's motivations to volunteer. One of these is called the motivation to volunteer (MTV) theory. This theory, developed by Clary and Snyder, asserts that people volunteer for many different reasons. Clary and Snyder went on to identify six general reasons people volunteer: to reduce negative feelings, because it is consistent with their values, for social interaction, to learn more about something, to gain experience, and to build self-esteem. In our example, this theory could be used as a framework for determining if the motivations of the college students included in the current study fall within these same categories (and, if so, which ones are most prominent) and whether other unique motivations exist.

Step 5: Developing Hypotheses

Once you have your topic and have a theoretical framework, you need to narrow your focus even further. In quantitative research, researchers often develop **hypotheses**. Hypotheses are predictions of what researchers expect to find that can be empirically verified. Hypotheses are often based on previous literature on the subject. Once the data have been collected, the hypotheses can be tested. In our current study focusing on motivations for volunteering among college students, one of our hypotheses could be:

Women will be more likely than men to volunteer.

Every hypothesis also has a **null hypothesis**. A null hypothesis is a statement of no relationship. In this case the null hypothesis would be:

Gender has no effect on volunteerism

We can test the hypothesis statistically and then, based on the results of the statistical analysis, determine if our hypothesis is supported or not. If it is supported, we reject the null hypothesis. If it is not statistically supported, we reject the hypothesis and accept the null. With hypotheses in social research we can find support but we cannot prove them because there is always a chance that what we have found is erroneous.

Step 6: Designing a Data Collection Instrument

A common quantitative method for students learning how to conduct research is surveying. If you have decided you will do a survey, you must design a survey questionnaire, determine how you will distribute it, and how you will acquire a sample. We have discussed the various methods of surveying and many types of samples; now let's focus on the construction of a survey questionnaire.

In all forms of surveys, good questions are essential. The list of questions for the survey is called the **survey questionnaire**. People often think that it is easy to write a questionnaire—that is until they try it for themselves! Writing good survey questions takes time and practice. There are many factors that must be considered and many types of survey questions that should be avoided.

Survey questions can be open-ended or close-ended. **Open-ended questions** allow participants to answer a question as they choose; no answer options are provided. Open-ended questions result in qualitative data that cannot be analyzed statistically and yield data that is difficult to make sense of. But they are ideal for situations when set answer options are not available or when you do not want people to be restricted in their responses. Although open-ended questions can result in rich data that can truly elicit what respondents think, they can also produce so much variation on a theme that analysis can be difficult. A sample of 300 college students might yield 300 different responses. A lot of open-ended questions also do not limit the respondent to just one word and this can result in an immense volume of text that must be analyzed. Because of this, most surveys consist primarily of close-ended questions. **Close-ended questions** are questions with set answer options provided. One type of close-ended question that is commonly used is called a **Likert scale** question. Likert scale questions are usually real statements about something that respondents are asked to agree or disagree with fully or partially. The responses allow a surveyor to measure various dimensions of a concept that is being studied. To avoid having respondents answer all of the questions in the same way, good survey questionnaire writers typically reverse the word order of some of the statements.

Surveys often contain both open- and close-ended questions. Typically, an open-ended question will be a follow-up question to a close-ended question. Follow-up questions like these (if they are asked only as a secondary question to an initial response) are called **contingency questions**. That is, they are contingent on a certain response having been provided in a previous question and apply to only certain respondents. An example will make this easier to understand:

1. Do you enjoy the classes that you are currently taking?

Yes
No

2. If yes, which classes are your favorites?

_____

Only respondents that answer "yes" to the initial question are asked to answer the follow-up (contingency) question. The first question is a close-ended

(continues on page 118)

Likert Scale Questions

Some examples of Likert scale questions are presented in the table below. In the questions with an asterisk, words order has been reversed to allow the researcher to identify survey questionnaires in which respondents simply checked off the boxes in one column without actually reading the questions.

Statement	Strongly Agree	Agree	Neutral	Disagree	Strongly Disagree
Homeless people are homeless because they are lazy.*					
There is plenty of work available for those who want it.*					
The government needs to do more to help the homeless in our society.					
People need to help themselves instead of relying on others.*					
Everyone has a basic right to housing.					
I would support a tax increase to help the homeless.					
As long as there are people in America without shelter, this country has failed to live up to its ideals.					
I feel bad for homeless people.					
Most homeless people would rather stay homeless than get a job.*					

Question Types to Avoid

Clear survey questions are essential to ensure high-quality data and prevent low response rates. Questions that are ambiguous or confusing or that include unfamiliar terminology can be very frustrating to respondents; often, they will simply stop trying to answer them. Some questions that seem appropriate and perfectly clear to the researcher are not as clear to respondents; others ask too many things. Imagine, for example, taking the following survey:

1. Do you think that the United States government should spend more money on education and less money on defense?   ( ) Yes   ( ) No
2. You wouldn't date someone with bad manners, would you?   ( ) Yes   ( ) No
3. How many close friends do you have?

   ( ) 0–1

   ( ) 1–2

   ( ) 3–4

   ( ) 5 or more

4. How many hours a day do you spend doing homework?

   ( ) 1– 2 hours

   ( ) 3–4 hours

   ( ) 5–6 hours

   ( ) more than 6 hours

How would you answer these questions? Each of them serves as an example of common errors in survey question construction. Question 1 (Do you think that the United States government should spend more money on education and less money on defense?) is known as a double-barreled question. A **double-barreled question** measures two concepts in one question—it is really two questions not one. A respondent may want to answer yes on the education component and no on the defense component or vice versa but there is no way to separate the answers and thus no way to answer the question! The simple solution is to break the double-barreled question into two individual questions, each of which measure only one concept.

Question 2 (You wouldn't date someone with bad manners, would you?) is a leading question. **Leading questions** are questions where the "correct" answer is implied in the question and the respondent is being led to it. It is essential not to guide respondents' answers. Good survey questions are designed to elicit real answers that reflect real situations or opinions; they do not prompt respondents to answer in certain ways.

Not only must questions be written clearly but response categories must also be clear and rational. Consider question 3 (How many close friends do you have?). The problem is not with the question but with the answer options because the options are not mutually exclusive. **Mutually exclusive** answer categories do not overlap with one another. A student with one close friend should not have to choose between the first answer option (0–1) and the second answer option (1–2). In mutually exclusive answer categories, the response can be indicated in one and only one option. A related issue is exhaustiveness. Questions with **exhaustive** answer categories are those in which all respondents have somewhere to indicate their appropriate response. The answer categories for question 4 (How many hours a day do you spend doing homework?) are not exhaustive because there may be respondents that typically spend 0 hours doing homework and have no place to indicate this response.

These questions can all be rewritten in ways that make them easy for respondent to understand and answer and, in turn, easier for the researcher to analyze the resulting data. Consider the following changes:

1a. Do you think that the United States government should spend more money on education?   ( ) Yes   ( ) No
1b. Do you think that the United States government should spend less money on defense?   ( ) Yes   ( ) No
2. How likely would you be to date someone with bad manners?

( ) very likely

( ) somewhat likely

( ) not likely at all

3. How many close friends do you have?

( ) 0

( ) 1–2

( ) 3–4

( ) 5 or more

4. How many hours a day do you spend doing homework?

( ) 0 hours

( ) 1–2 hours

( ) 3–4 hours

( ) 5–6 hours

( ) more than 6 hours

(continued from page 115)
question whereas the second is open-ended. This combination allows for a more thorough analysis. From the first question we can determine what percentage of students in our sample enjoy their classes. From the second question we can determine which classes are listed most frequently as the respondents' favorites.

An excellent way to determine if your questionnaire makes sense to potential participants is to conduct a **pretest**. A pretest consists of administering your questionnaire to a few people that fit your target demographic and soliciting them for feedback on the questionnaire. The pretest can help you assess whether your questions are clear, whether they have the appropriate answer categories, and whether they are eliciting the type of information that you want to collect. The results can help you refine the questionnaire before you begin collecting real data for your study.

In qualitative research, structured questions are often used as a means of collecting data. These questions could be used in one-on-one interviews, group interviews, or focus groups. You can develop a list of questions that will allow you to explore your topic in depth with respondents. As in quantitative research, you can pretest these questions to ensure that they are clear and that they elicit the appropriate information. This list of questions will serve as a guide to the interviewer or moderator during the interview or focus group session.

Step 7: Collecting Data

Once you have chosen your method for data collection, finalized data collection instrument, and obtained IRB approval, it is time to collect data. While planning your method you will have identified how you will get your participants. The people that participate in your research will be your sample.

Oftentimes researchers will not collect their own data, relying instead on secondary data analysis. As previously noted, secondary data analysis is the analysis of data that were previously collected by someone else. Typically secondary data are quantitative although some qualitative secondary data are available for analysis. Because the data have already been collected, using secondary data is an immense time saver. One clear advantage to using secondary data is that it facilitates researchers in accessing large volumes of data, even if resources are limited. If you are interested in nationwide data, for example, you may not have the means (resources) necessary to collect that data. Using secondary data solves this problem. Many data sets come from government entities such as the U.S. Census Bureau and are available to anyone. There are also data sets available on virtually every topic imaginable. These data sets are generally inexpensive; if your school or university subscribes to the appropriate service or data archive, they are often free.

There are several national data sets that are particularly popular for use in secondary data analysis. One is the General Social Survey (GSS). The GSS is a nationally representative quantitative survey of American adults, which measures demographic information and a wide range of behaviors and attitudes. Many of the standard questions have been asked in the same way since 1972, the first year the GSS was administered. This allows researchers to conduct longitudinal analyses with secondary data.

Although secondary data analysis is a very popular form of research that possesses many advantages compared to other methods, there are some drawbacks. The most significant of these is the fact that the data were collected by someone else. This means the researcher cannot ensure that the data quality is high or that the data entry was done correctly. Oftentimes researchers using secondary data will find themselves wondering why certain questions were not included, or they may not like how certain questions were worded. Unfortunately, there is nothing that can be done to correct this. Secondary data is what it is. Nonetheless, with the myriad of datasets available, it remains a popular and efficient way to conduct research.

Step 8: Analyzing Data

If the data you collected are quantitative then you will analyze them statistically. If the data are qualitative, then you will most likely code the data for the themes. To do this, interviews or focus group sessions must first be transcribed. Once you have a transcription, you can go line by line and assign codes to the data. These codes are simply ways to categorize and make sense of the data. For example, let's suppose that 20 college students were interviewed after the conclusion of their first semesters and asked, "Now that you have completed your first semester of college, what would you like to work on for next semester to make yourself a better student?"

Here are their answers:

Finding internships to help me get experience.
Talk to an advisor about opportunities in my potential career field.
Ask if my professor has any research opportunities.
Introduce myself to my professors so they know who I am.
Get an agenda book and write down when all of my assignments are
  due.
Dedicate more time to studying.
Research offices on campus that can help me become employable after
  I graduate.
Try to find a job that connects to my major.
Go to a club meeting.
Find a tutor on campus.
Join a club to meet new people.

Go to a workshop on job interviews and resume writing.
Volunteer for an event on campus.
Actually go to class and take notes.
Start a club with my friends.
Go to a club meeting.
Ask my professor questions about material I don't understand.
Party less and study more.
Email my professor whenever I have a problem.
Find someone to shadow to see if I really want to be a doctor.
Start a team with my friends and play an intramural sport.

To code the data, we will have to organize these responses into categories:

Gaining Experience
Finding internships to help me get experience.
Talk to an advisor about opportunities in my potential career field.
Research offices on campus that can help me become employed after
    I graduate.
Try to find a job that connects to my major.

Study Habits/Time Management
Get an agenda book and write down when all of my assignments are due.
Dedicate more time to studying.
Find a tutor on campus.
Party less and study more.
Actually go to class and take notes.

Organization Involvement
Join a club to meet new people.
Volunteer for an event on campus.
Start a club with my friends.
Start a team with my friends and play an intramural sport.
Go to a club meeting.

Professor Interaction
Ask my professor questions about material I don't understand.
Introduce myself to my professors so they know who I am.
Ask if my professor has any research opportunities.
Email my professor whenever I have a problem.

This is not the only way to code these data. Your codes may be different. You may have more or fewer categories, different categories, or categorize responses differently. That is fine as long you are being systematic in your coding and clear about how and why you coded responses as you did. This helps you to structure your data and your research and also allows others to see how your data were coded.

Step 9: Writing up the Results of Analysis
The results section presents all relevant findings from the analyses that you conducted as a part of your research study. In a quantitative study this section usually contains tables showing the results of statistical tests that were performed to test the hypotheses set forth in the study. In addition, researchers will write about the results of their statistical tests. For qualitative studies, this section will discuss what themes were uncovered through the coding process. Excerpts from interview or focus group sessions are included in this section to support the claims made by the researcher. In other words, the data consist of text, not numbers or statistics.

Step 10: Writing a Conclusion
The conclusion of a research project connects the findings (or results) from the particular study to the broader realm of research. This is where you can discuss whether your hypotheses were supported. Did you find what you expected to find based on your review of the literature? How does your study add to what we know about your topic? How do the findings impact what we know about this topic? What are the implications of the findings? Conclusions and result sections are often viewed as the same thing, but they are quite different. Whereas results present the actual analysis of the study, the conclusion section will put the analysis in context and discuss what the analysis means in the bigger picture.

Because there is no such thing as a perfect study, researchers usually include in their conclusion a discussion of limitations. Some common limitations are presenting research that was conducted using a sample that is not representative or that is quite small. It is important for the researcher to acknowledge the limitations of a study. Including limitations can in fact helps direct future research by prompting other researchers to design studies that help to correct or circumvent certain limitations.

Studies often also make explicit recommendations for future research. This can include suggesting different methods that might be used to further explore an issue or recommending how the study might be applied to different groups of people. For example, in our volunteerism study we discussed a quantitative study examining motivations for volunteering among young people. Future researchers may benefit from studying this topic in a qualitative way (for example, conducting interviews with young people who do volunteer) to acquire a better understanding of the motivations that impact behavior (in this case, volunteering).

Step 11: Preparing the Final Paper

Just as research follows a basic design, so too does a research paper. Typically a paper consists of these main sections: introduction, literature review, methods, results, and conclusion. There are many variations of course, but these are the key sections usually included. The introduction serves as a way to acquaint the reader with the topic. The literature review as you already know is a discussion of previous work in your topic area. The methods section will explain what method(s) you used to conduct your research. It will also include a discussion of your sample, if applicable, and a discussion of your data analysis techniques. A well written methods section should be so clearly written that readers will have no questions as to how the study was conducted and can even replicate it. Once your methods have been described clearly, it is time to share your results and discuss the major implications and significance of your findings.

Your paper should end with a list of references. The reference page will consist of citations of all of the works that you cited throughout your paper. Reference pages are important not only to prevent suspicion of plagiarism but also as a tool for other researchers. A reference section can often be one of the most helpful parts of a paper for other researchers interested in a similar topic as it informs researchers about studies that have been done to date.

The last thing you might do in writing a research paper is to prepare an **abstract,** a short summary of a research study which typically precedes the full article about the research in a publication. Abstracts are discussed last here as they are usually written after an entire study has been completed. The typical abstract ranges from 150 to 250 words and broadly summarizes the entire study. When writing an abstract, a researcher usually starts with two sentences introducing the topic, followed by a brief discussion of the methods and sample, and finally, the results. To conclude their abstract, some researchers explain why their study is significant, although this is an optional step.

Abstracts are great way to let readers know if a particular study is relevant to their own work without obligating them to read 20 to 40 pages of material. These summaries can also give prospective researchers an overview of how others have examined the topic and allow them to see what holes need to be filled. Along with the sources included in your literature review, abstracts serve as reminders about what a particular study did so others do not have to go through the entire study process again.

SUMMARY

Although conducting a research project for the first time can be daunting, it is also very exciting. This chapter presented the outline of a typical study, although variations on this process and structure exist. All projects are different, and researchers are not tied to a particular format. Nevertheless, many articles follow this general outline because it is a concise and clear way to present research. Developing research skills takes time and practice. Even experienced researchers learn something new each time they conduct a new study. Research is the basis of sociology and is how we go about explaining the social world in a systematic and in-depth way. Good research is invaluable.

Further Reading

American Sociological Association Style Guide. 4th ed. Washington, D.C.: American Sociological Association, 2010.

Galvan, Jose L.. *Writing Literature Reviews: A Guide for Students of the Social and Behavioral Sciences.* 3rd ed. Glendale, Calif.: Pyrczak, 2005.

Johnson, William A.. *The Sociology Student Writer's Manual.* 6th ed. Upper Saddle River, N.J.: Prentice Hall, 2010.

Matson, Ronald R. *The Spirit of Sociology: A Reader.* 3rd ed. Boston: Allyn & Bacon, 2010.

GLOSSARY

abstract A short summary of a research study.

annotated bibliography A list of summaries of articles on a particular topic.

anonymous When researcher(s) or other people who either take part in the data collection process and read the findings do not know the identity of the participants and their specific responses.

applied sociology A facet of sociology in which researchers use sociological methods and theories outside of academia.

atheoretical A term used to describe something that lacks a theoretical grounding. This term is mostly used to describe scientific studies.

Audio Computer Assisted Self-Interviewing (ACASI) A form of survey research that uses new technology to collect data (typically on topics of sensitive nature) and to lessen the social desirability effect.

authority Refers to those scholars that have become recognized as experts on certain topics or in specific areas of study.

autoethnography An autobiographical account of a writer's life in which lived experience is explored in depth.

average The sum of all the responses divided by the number of responses. See *mean*.

The Belmont Report A report that presents the basic ethical principles and guidelines that researchers must follow when conducting research.

bias Something that occurs when there is a distortion or slanted viewpoint that guides people to answer a question a certain way or produce a sought after result.

blind experiment An experiment in which subjects do not know if they are in the group that is being exposed to the variable being measured (the treatment group) or not (the control group).

breaching experiments A method used in ethnomethodological studies that measures or examines the reaction of people when someone violates established cultural expectations of behavior or social norm.

case study A qualitative research method that involves the study of a single group, event, or person.

causality Investigating cause and effect.

census A survey that collects data from all members of a population.

citation Provides a reference to the source of the information. If works of others are presented without citations, it is a form of plagiarism (see *plagiarism*).

clickers Wireless, handheld devices that allow users to instantly register their response to a posed question.

close-ended question A question with set answer options provided.

code sheet A list of all of the elements in a sample and the results of the coding done by the researcher (see *Coding*).

coding The way information is quantified and labeled. Researchers determine what to code for before beginning the actual coding process.

cohort study A longitudinal study that observes or studies a certain group or population of people over a period of time and assesses the changes in their attitudes or beliefs (see *Longitudinal*).

Computer Assisted Telephone Interviewing (CATI) A process in which telephone surveyors read questions from a computer screen and enter each respondent's answers into a data collection program, which eliminates the need for data entry later.

confidentiality When a researcher knows the identity the participants of his or her study and knows each of their specific responses and personal information but promises not to disclose any of this information to anyone other than the research team. Note that confidentiality is not the same as anonymity (see *Anonymous*).

constant A variable that has the same value and does not change from one observation to another.

content analysis The systematic analysis of social artifacts.

content validity A way to gauge how fully a concept is measured.

contingency question A follow-up question that is based on a participant's response to a previous question.

convenience sample A sample that consists of people who are available to the researcher simply because they are at the location where the sampling is taking place.

conversation analysis Analysis that uses audio or video recordings or written transcripts of naturally occurring conversations as a source of data. The researcher is not a participant in these conversations.

correlation An association between two variables.

cost-benefit analysis An assessment of the value of a program or policy.

covert participation A study in which a researcher does not tell the others in a group that he or she is conducting research (see *participant observation*).

criterion validity Validity that seeks to confirm that two measures of the same social phenomenon relate to one another.

critical instance case study A case study that examines a specific phenomenon of rare interest or challenges an extremely generalized widespread claim.

cross-sectional Research that is conducted at and represents one point in time. This type of study contrasts with a *longitudinal* study.

data Information organized for analysis.

debriefing Occurs when a researcher talks to the participants of a project about their experiences while partaking in his or her study. This usually takes place if there is a chance that taking part in the study has somehow harmed the participants.

deception Takes place in studies that do not fully explain to participants the purpose of the study in its entirety or misleads participants into thinking that the study is measuring something other than was explained to them.

deductive Research that starts with a theory of a social phenomenon that lays the foundation for the study and then leads to the formation of a research question and hypotheses. After that, an experiment is conducted during which data is collected and analyzed.

descriptive study Research that seeks to describe a social phenomenon of interest; typically the first studies done on a particular topic.

dependent variables A variable that is predicted to depend on or be caused by the *independent variable*.

dispersion A statistical term that refers to how data points are scattered around a certain value, like the mean or the median.

double-barreled question A survey question that measures two concepts at once.

double-blind experiment An experiment design in which neither the subjects nor the researchers know which groups (treatment of control) subjects have been assigned to.

ecological fallacy An error in reasoning which occurs when incorrect assumptions about an individual are made based on findings about the group the individual belongs to or is associated with.

ethnography A qualitative method; the systematic study of human cultures.

ethnomethodology A research method that examines how people in a society produce and organize interaction in their daily lives. Two methods that have resulted from this are *breaching experiments* and *conversation analysis*.

evaluation research Research that examines the effectiveness of policies and programs, and involves outcome measures or goals. This type of research is usually required for any federally funded program.

exhaustive When answer options presented in survey questions cover all possible answer options.

experiment A method used in most scientific research. When done properly, an experiment can test hypotheses in a pure environment free from outside influences. Although it is an ideal method, sociological studies do not take place in a laboratory.

explanatory study A research study that focuses on establishing causal relationships and explanations for people's behaviors, beliefs. or attitudes.

explicit information Information that is easily transmitted to others, usually in written form. This can be found in *participant observation*.

exploratory case study A case study that is initiated to help explore any type of phenomenon before a large-scale examination begins.

exploratory study A research study that focuses on meaning, motivations for behavior.

external validity The ability of the results of a study to generalize beyond the sample and environment in the study.

face validity Validity that ensures that the measure being used is suitable to the concept being studied.

focus group A guided, group discussion on a topic of interest.

formative evaluation An evaluation that assesses the worth of a program or policy before or during its implementation. These types of evaluations may help shape the way a program is delivered or even help determine what types of programs or policies should be implemented in the first place (see *evaluation research*).

frequency distribution   A statistical tabulation of the values that a variable takes.

gatekeeper   A person who provides a researcher access to a group. The gatekeeper can help assure other group members that the researcher is someone who can be allowed in, putting other members at ease or legitimating the researcher as someone who can be considered one of them.

generalizability   The ability to take findings from a sample and apply them to the larger population that the sample was drawn from.

Global Information Systems (GIS)   A system that obtains, keeps, analyzes, and displays data that is associated with location.

group administered   A technique for recruiting study participants which involves personally distributing surveys to a large group of people all at once in a setting such as a university classroom or a workplace.

group dynamic   A way of thinking (within a group of participants) about a particular issue that the others may never have considered. The discussion that ensues will give clues as to why people hold the views that they do.

guiding questions   A list of questions that steer or direct a conversation. Used in focus groups and interviews.

haphazard sampling   Acquiring artifacts to study because they are easily accessible or available; not a systematic way to sample.

Hawthorne Effect   The tendency of subjects to act differently when they know they are being studied, especially if they think they have been singled out for some experimental treatment.

historical research   A research method that uses existing historical documents in an analysis of past events in order to inform current life.

hypotheses   Predictions of what researchers expect to find.

illogical reasoning   Research conclusions that are not empirically justified.

illustrative case study   A case study that is used when trying to describe an specific event or specific situation (see *case study*).

impact evaluation   An evaluation that measures not just the intended and stated outcomes, but the greater potential impact the program or policy had, even if it was unintended (see *evaluation research*).

implementation evaluation   An important type of evaluation research that focuses on the way a program or policy was implemented (see *evaluation research*).

implied consent   A situation in which the participation of the individual counts as the consent that is based on the premise that because the individual continues to participate in a study, he or she has agreed to be included. This type of consent works in mail and phone surveys.

incentives Inducements to encourage people to participate in research.

independent variable A variable in which the values are already set and influence the *dependent variable.*

inductive Research that creates a theory from what is revealed by the data. It is usually seen in qualitative research.

informed consent Consent from participants who have been informed what is required of them as they part in the study and have also been informed about any possible risks involved.

Institutional Review Boards (IRBs) Professional panels that review research plans for research that involves human subjects.

Intercoder Reliability (ICR) Having more than one person code the artifacts on the same dimensions and then comparing the results.

internal validity The right to assert that the changes in an independent variable produced a certain outcome.

intersubjectivity A researcher's own interpretation of data that includes interviews, interaction, and observations.

interval A level of measurement in which you know or can measure the difference between categories.

intervening variables Variables that might have an impact on the relationship between an independent and a dependent variable.

intervention Manipulation of the variable of interest, used in experiments.

latent content The underlying meaning of the subject matter being examined. This type of content can be found in content analysis studies.

leading question A question in which the "correct" answer is implied in the question and the respondent is being led to it.

Likert scale A question that usually presents statements to which a respondent can express different levels of agreement or disagreement.

literature review An essay that discusses previous research articles about a particular research topic.

longitudinal A type of study in which the research conducted is completed over time or in waves.

manifest content The apparent meaning of the subject matter being examined. This kind of content can be found in content analysis studies.

mean The average of a set of data. To calculate the mean you simply add up all of the responses and divide by the number of responses.

measurement The dimension or the quantity of something.

median The midpoint of a frequency distribution.

mixed methods Combining different methodologies for research.

moderator The role of the researcher in focus groups as a facilitator during group discussion among study participants.

mode The most common value in a frequency distribution.

modes The main ways that surveys can be administered (via mail, telephone, Internet, in person, and group administered).

multimethod The use of two or more research methods in a research study.

mutually exclusive Answer categories that do not overlap with one another so a participant's response can be indicated in one and only one option.

needs assessment A process of determining what gaps or needs are present in the environment being studied; a type of evaluation research.

negative correlation A correlation in which the value of the independent variable increases while the value of the dependent variable decreases or vice versa.

nominal A level of measurement in which the categories describe the data.

null hypothesis A statement of no relationship.

observation Systematically noticing details within an environment. It is the basis of all scientific research and an essential part of qualitative studies.

open-ended question A question that allows the participant to answer in the way he or she chooses.

operational definition Explains a concept or variable in terms of the operations that will be used to measure that concept, that is, the precise specification of the decision rule or rules that will be used to assign numbers to represent the variable properties of the phenomenon.

operationalization The process of providing a clear and concise definition that allows for a concept or variable to be measured.

ordinal A level of measurement in which you cannot measure the difference between categories.

outcome evaluation An evaluation that focuses on the stated outcomes the program or policy was designed to meet. The purpose of the outcome evaluation is to determine if there was a positive change as a result of the program or policy being implemented (see *evaluation research*).

overgeneralization Sweeping conclusions based on limited observations.

overt participation When the researcher tells others in a group being studied that he or she is conducting research (see *participant observation*).

panel studies A type of longitudinal study that uses the same sample in every data collection episode.

Participatory Action Research (PAR)   A research method in which the researcher integrates himself into a group under study. The researcher's goal is to enact change.

participation observation   A method of inquiry where the researcher is an active participant in a social setting.

peer review   Professional evaluation of a researcher's work.

photoethnography   A research method that involves giving participants a camera so they can take photos on a particular topic. These photos are printed and then participants are interviewed about the photos to determine what they mean and why they are important.

plagiarism   A term used to describe the theft of written intellectual thought. It can result in severe academic and professional consequences, including expulsion from school or termination from a job.

population   The group of people that a sample will be derived from.

positive correlation   A correlation in which the values of the independent and dependent variables both increase (or decrease).

pretest   Testing a questionnaire prior to data collection.

probability   The likelihood that something will occur.

probe   A follow-up question designed to elicit more information from a participant in a research study.

purposive sample   A nonprobability sample in which sample members are selected to fulfill the purpose of a study.

qualitative research   Research that uses contextual data to produce a deep understanding of a social phenomenon.

quantitative research   Research that relies on statistics to make generalizations about the subject matter of interest.

quasi-experimental design   A research design similar to a true experiment in that a treatment and a comparison group are compared. However, group members are not randomly assigned to these two groups.

quota sample   A nonprobability sample in which a researcher knows the demographics of the population.

ratio   A level of measurement in which the difference between categories is known or can be measured. An absolute zero point exists on the scale.

reliability   Research that will produce the same results when it is repeated.

replication study   A study that will be the same as one previously conducted. The only difference will be the specific people involved in the research. It is used to show that the findings in one study were not a fluke or that the findings hold across different groups of people or in different circumstances.

research   A process of systematic observations.

research question   The question that a research study will attempt to answer.

response rate   The number of people who participate out of the total number of people who were asked to participate.

response set tendencies   Ways in which respondents tend to answer questions regardless of the question content. An example of this would be a respondent answering yes to all of the yes or no questions.

risk to subjects   The potential risks associated when participating in a research study.

sampling frame   The list of all of the elements in the population.

secondary data analysis   Analysis of data that were collected by someone else.

selective observation   What occurs when researchers purposefully seek out observations that confirm their preexisting beliefs or opinions.

self-administered questionnaire   A questionnaire that is out by respondents themselves. Mail surveys are an example.

simple random sample   A sample in which every member of the population has an equal chance of being selected.

skip logic   A pattern used in surveys directs respondents to answer or skip questions in a series, depending on an answer option previously selected.

snowball sampling   A nonprobability sample where people who are part of the sample are asked to help the researcher by recruiting other people to participate in the same study.

social artifacts   Television shows, movies, song lyrics, music videos, speeches, book genres and art, etc., that can be analyzed *unobtrusively*, under the method of *content analysis*.

social desirability   A tendency by respondents to give answers that are socially acceptable instead of answers that are honest.

sociological imagination   A term coined by C. Wright Mills that refers to the process of thinking about the connections between the things we have experienced and the larger society in which we live.

spurious   A term used to describe when causation can be apparent but it is false. This happens when the observed causal relationship can be explained by a third variable.

stakeholders Individuals, groups, or organizations who have a vested interest in a program or policy that is being evaluated.

statistics A field of study within mathematics that deals with the collection, analysis, and interpretation of quantitative data.

stratified sampling A researcher's plans to focus on specific social groups within the *sample* or target *population* before conducting research.

summative evaluation Evaluation that focuses on the outcomes of programs or policies. Summative evaluations occur after a program or policy has been implemented and measures the manner in which it was implemented and its overall effectiveness (see *evaluation research*).

survey fatigue A term used to explain potential respondents who have received so many requests to participate in surveys that they are no longer willing to do so.

survival bias A phenomenon that occurs when some individual *social artifacts* are more available than others in the entire population.

survey questionnaire The list of questions for the survey.

systematic sample A sampling method in which every nth case is selected.

tacit information Knowledge taken for granted by those who possess is and is difficult to transmit to others.

theory A researcher's systematic speculations.

theory-driven evaluation A type of evaluation that seeks to ascertain what the underlying theory of a particular program is and if that underlying theory is logical given what we know about the issue that the program focuses on.

tradition Written knowledge that has been published to date.

transcription A written copy of an audio or video recording.

trend study A type of longitudinal study that focuses on a specific topic and asks the same or very similar questions over time. Different respondents are chosen to answer the questions each time.

triangulation Examining the same topic using several different methods or approaches. Triangulation is based on a mathematical principle.

unit of analysis What or whom is being researched.

unobtrusive measures A research method that does not require interaction with respondents.

validity Measurements or questions that must measure what they are intended to measure.

variable A grouping of logical attributes that will vary depending on other factors.

windshield survey A research method during which researchers observe the environment through the windshield of a vehicle or by walking through an environment; frequently used in studies that require assessment of neighborhoods or communities.

BIBLIOGRAPHY

Berg, Bruce L. *Qualitative Research Methods for the Social Sciences*. 6th ed. Boston: Pearson/Allyn & Bacon, 2007.

DeWalt, Kathleen Musante, and Billie R. DeWalt. *Participant Observation: A Guide for Fieldworkers*. 2nd ed. Lanham, Md.: Rowman & Littlefield, MD., 2011.

Galvan, Jose L. *Writing Literature Reviews: A Guide for Students of the Social and Behavioral Sciences*. 3rd ed. Glendale, Calif.: Pyrczak, 2005.

Healey, Joseph. *The Essentials of Statistics*. 2nd ed. Belmont, Calif.: Wadsworth, 2010.

Lofland, John. *Analyzing Social Settings: A Guide to Qualitative Observation and Analysis*. 4th ed. Belmont, Calif.: Wadsworth/Thomson Learning, 2006.

Marsden, Peter V., and James D. Wright. *Handbook of Survey Research*. 2nd ed. Bingley, UK: Emerald, 2010.

Merton, Robert King. *Social Theory and Social Structure*. New York: Free Press, 1968.

Miller, Delbert C., and Neil J. Salkind. *Handbook of Research Design and Social Measurement*. 6th ed. Thousand Oaks, Calif.: Sage Publications, 2002.

Mills, C. Wright. *The Sociological Imagination*. Oxford, England: Oxford University Press, 1968.

Riffe, Daniel, Stephen Lacy, and Frederick Fico. *Analyzing Media Messages: Using Quantitative Content Analysis in Research*. 2nd ed. Mahwah, N.J.: Lawrence Erlbaum, 2005.

Rossi, Peter H., Mark W. Lipsey, and Howard E. Freeman. *Evaluation: A Systematic Approach*. 7th ed. Thousand Oaks, Calif.: Sage, 2003.

Stark, Laura. *Behind Closed Doors: IRBs and the Making of Ethical Research*. Chicago: The University of Chicago Press, 2011.

INDEX